With love from the good looking one ....!

WARE AND HERTFORD

Robert and Clive

The authors and publishers would wish to express their
appreciation for the kind donations received
to subsidise the production of this book

The Sponsors are

The Environmental Service of the Hertfordshire County Council
The Robert Kiln Charitable Trust
Glaxo
Mr and Mrs R J Kiln
The Hertfordshire Archaeological Trust
Hertford Town Council

FRONTISPIECE: *Upper* – Saxon strapend/clasp from the Secret Garden site, Ware (Full size)
Lower – Late Saxon jug from Railway Street, Hertford ($\frac{1}{4}$ size)

WARE

AND

HERTFORD

The story of two towns
from
birth to middle age

R.J.KILN and C.R.PARTRIDGE

Castlemead
PUBLICATIONS
WELWYN GARDEN CITY

First published 1995

CASTLEMEAD PUBLICATIONS
12, Little Mundells
Welwyn Garden City
Hertfordshire AL7 1EW

Proprietors: Ward's Publishing Services

ISBN 0 948555 37 8

© R.J.Kiln and C.R.Partridge 1994

British Library Cataloguing In Publication Data

A catalogue record for this book is available from the British Library

Phototypeset in 11/13pt Palatino by Intype, London.
Printed and bound in Great Britain by
The Bath Press, Avon.

Preface

Over the past twenty-five years a great deal of archaeological work has been carried out both in the two towns and in the surrounding countryside. Much of this is still unpublished and it is intended that this book will provide a summary of that work and of the exciting discoveries made. It also offers our theories on how and why the two towns were formed and grew where they did. Of course it is speculative in places and we hope written in a way that will appeal to the general reader, not just archaeologists and historians. We feel it is right that people should have access to this knowledge, much of which, after all, was gained by public money or voluntary effort on the part of many of the towns' citizens. We hope that at least the major unpublished excavations will appear in the not too distant future. Any monies remaining from the sale of this book will be put towards a fund to aid such publication. In the meantime we feel that this book will help to stimulate interest about both the towns. Above all, we trust that you will enjoy reading it; after all, that is the main reason we have taken it upon ourselves to write it. The title Ware and Hertford was chosen without disrespect for Hertford, but simply because Ware is, on present knowledge, by far the older of the two towns and, for a good part of the period we are discussing, the more important.

Acknowledgements

We would like to acknowledge the help and encouragement we have received from many people in the production of this book, including the following:

The financial sponsors of the project, without whose generous contributions the production of this book would not have been possible and certainly not at the price it is available to the public. They are listed individually at the front of the book. Our production editor, Elisabeth Barratt, for her own contributions to the story and for much of the original editing and all the drafting and redrafting of the final typescript and printers' discs. Our publishers Castlemead for taking on board the idea and to Alan Ward, Susan Lee and their staff for all their help and patience. Castlemead's editor Michael Coultas for his expertise, suggestions and improvements. Margaret Archer for typing and retyping many of the original drafts. Letty Kiln for reading it in draft and for her helpful suggestions. Peter Walne, for his help with the problem of the Alien Benedictine Priory at Ware and suggesting the article which forms Appendix C. Ware and Hertford Town Councils for allowing us to use the town crests on the front cover design. Graham Edwards for providing us with a copy of the late Rev. Gill's booklet on St Andrews church. Rev. Colin Weale for his notes on St Leonard's, Bengeo. Hester Cooper-Reade and the Hertfordshire Archaeological Trust for notes and suggestions on the excavations at Millbridge and for the use of photographs from their archives and Adrian Havercroft for help with the List of Excavations. Glaxo UK for permission to use the aerial photograph of Allen & Hanbury's in 1950 and the use of their internal plan of the complex. Hertford Museum for the use of photographs. Ware Museum for access to material for photography. The *Hertfordshire Mercury* for publicity and help with the distribution of the book. Joy Norris for her excellent reconstructions, reproduced as Colour Plates I-II and V-VIII. Tony Meadows for permission to use his painting of the Foxholes Farm corndryers (Colour Plate III). Sal Garfi for Appendix A and allowing the use of some of his plans from his Survey. The Essex Numismatic Society for permission to use the late David Fish's article for Appendix B. East Hertfordshire Archaeological Society for permission to use part of an article by the late Rev. Harry P. Pollard from their *Transactions* as Appendix C, and particularly for kindly agreeing to act as agents for handling the financial matters and disbursements for this book. And finally Richard Wilson for Appendix D.

Contents

List of Figures

List of Colour Plates

List of Plates

ix

Introduction

As the crow flies Hertford and Ware lie approximately twenty miles due north of London Bridge. For towns so close to the ever expanding sprawl of outer London they have both managed, in a remarkable degree, to preserve their identity and original street plans. They have, in the main, escaped the horrors of wholesale redevelopment.

The two towns lie cheek by jowl in the Lea Valley. Inevitably they have interacted one upon the other and at times the rivalry has been intense. It seems logical, given the closely interrelated histories of the towns over many centuries, that they should be chronicled together in a single volume.

In the last century and the first half of this one, Hertford and Ware were surrounded by large private estates which have been kept relatively intact and undeveloped. The marshy, unstable geology of the river valley has also helped to prevent the spread of building along the valley floor. Since the Second World War the major developments have taken place along the two major communication corridors with London; in the east the Lea and Stort Valley and to the west the line of the A1 trunk road and main railway line through Hatfield and Stevenage. The development of new towns followed these routes: Harlow, Stevenage, Welwyn Garden City and Hatfield are the obvious examples.

It is only since 1965 and, in particular, after 1980 that our towns have undergone any significant degree of redevelopment; notwithstanding this fact, a fast rail service to London is still lacking. Both towns are fortunate to have very active Civic Societies which have prevented more wanton destruction of the old town layouts. However, the arrival of the M25 to the south heralds a new era of potential threat. The largely unspoilt countryside and the convenience of the area, north to the Lea, has very obvious attractions as a dormitory for London.

HERTFORD

With one or two exceptions, rebuilding in the town centre has been piece-meal and in many cases this has allowed some amount of archaeological investigation before and during construction work. Most of this investigation was necessarily of a rescue nature which, at best, provides an incomplete picture and at worst affords the merest peepholes into the past. Exceptions to this piecemeal work were the construction of the inner relief road in the early 1960s, which cut a swathe through the southern half of the town and across part of its western side. Unfortunately, only very minor archaeological investigation could be carried out during the construction of this disastrous piece of vandalism.

The other development was the Bircherley Green Precinct in the centre of town. Here the original planned development was reduced in its extent due to local pressure. During this redevelopment a reasonable amount of archaeological excavation and recording was carried out by the Hart Archaeological Unit; the results have provided a significant addition to our knowledge of Saxon Hertford south of the Lea. Work has been continued by the Hertfordshire Archaeological Trust on a number of sites, mainly north of the Lea; this work has established the existence of at least some Roman and pre-Roman Iron Age occupation in the general area of the riverside at Millbridge and St Andrews Street.

WARE

The A10 bypassing of Ware, unlike the Hertford relief road, was well outside the town centre and caused little destruction of historical significance. The more recent extensive redevelopment of areas to the east of the Amwell End Bridge have, luckily, been mostly outside the boundaries of Ware's early development.

The most significant development in Ware has undoubtedly been that on the old Allen & Hanbury site. The new owners, Glaxo UK, have carried out a rolling programme of redevelopment which, sadly, has seen the demise of a large part of the Roman town, the underlying Iron Age settlement and the important Mesolithic features.

Commendably, firstly Allen & Hanbury and later on Glaxo acknowledged their public responsibility to allow the recovery and recording of evidence before it was destroyed. Thus between 1976 and 1985 the Hart Archaeological Unit carried out a number of important excavations in advance of development. These excavations firmly established the presence of a small Roman town which partly overlies substantial remains of Late Iron Age date. The uncovering of important Mesolithic occupation, with structural remains and flintwork dating to the fifth/sixth century BC, was an unexpected bonus.

Remains of a late Saxon settlement was found in the Baldock Street area. A Saxon *sceatta* (a small silver coin) was discovered during excavations in

West Street. Metalwork and grass-tempered pottery have been found on other sites.

Other phases of work have investigated the sites of the Alien Benedictine Priory and the Franciscan Friary. In more recent years this work of recovery and recording has been continued by the Hertfordshire Archaeological Trust, again on the Glaxo site, the Secret Garden site and several smaller investigations in various parts of the town.

From the foregoing it will be obvious that we are now in a position to make a respectable attempt at unravelling the early history of the towns; how they originated and how they relate to each other in terms of geology, topography and history. There are still gaps and areas of uncertainty in our knowledge and understanding of the two towns. It should be borne in mind that much is still open to debate and reinterpretation, therefore some major discovery, or even a chance find, could well alter our thinking and perhaps radically change the picture that is presented here.

1
Geology and Geography

In geological terms, the forming of this part of England happened fairly recently. It starts around sixty million years ago when the whole south-eastern part of England and north-eastern France was covered by water. This, at first, was a shallow muddy sea which settled and formed a layer of fine clay. Then for thirty million years this sea remained tranquil. For aeons the bodies of dead sea creatures settled like snowflakes, falling through the clear waters to form layer upon layer of shells and bony skeletons. In time, with decay and the enormous weight of water pushing down, this detritus was crushed and solidified to form the soft rock we now call chalk; this built up to hundreds of feet thick in some places and lies over the clay layer. From the myriad remains of sponges and many other sea creatures the process of decay produced silica. Under pressure this silica was squeezed out to form little pools. When compressed by the millions of tons of chalk above and with the heat from the earth's core below, this silica solidified into the very hard substance we now know as flint.

Later on the land was gradually pushed up and the chalk was covered once more by the mud, sands and gravels of a shallower sea and the outflow of rivers draining into it. Later still, the land rose until it was above the sea level. Around fifteen to twenty million years ago the African Continent moved north and collided with Southern Europe. The shock caused the huge buckling that raised the Alps and the Pyrenees. The ripples of this great upheaval reached our area and caused the chalk to bend with wave-like contortions. The crests of these waves form the chalk hills of the North and South Downs and the Chilterns, with the trough between forming what we call the London Basin. Over the years the higher chalk was worn away in places. But new layers of sand, mud and gravel, laid down by rivers, lakes and outwash from melting glaciers was often deposited on top.

Originally the Weald of Kent and Sussex was a high spot, but erosion of the softer chalk areas has left the North and South scarps of the Downs facing each other across the earlier, harder rocks of the Weald. Likewise the chalk to the north of the Chilterns has been worn away leaving the steep scarp face of the Chilterns facing roughly to the north-west. Hertford and

Ware lie towards the northern part of the London Basin. In fact, they lie on the 'dip slope' of the Chilterns (Fig. 1).

Since the chalk was first folded, some twenty million years or so ago, the process of filling the trough of the London Basin has gone on. At times the rivers, like the Thames and the Lea, have been wide and slow moving. At other times the rivers have been fast moving and abrasive, cutting down deeply into the soft alluvial deposits. The succeeding periods of filling and cutting can be seen today as terraces along the valley sides.

There was a profound change in the climatic conditions some four million years ago resulting in a series of ice ages. At their greatest extent the ice caps, or Glaciers as we call them, spread from Scandinavia across the North Sea to reach eastern England and the ice caps in Scotland and the Pennines extended south. At times this ice sheet almost reached our area, but Hertfordshire generally was about its most southerly extent.

One major result was that the river Thames, which had originally flowed directly east through Hertford and Ware to the North Sea, became blocked by ice. The dammed waters formed a large lake before overflowing and cutting a new channel through the Goring Gap, to flow in its present course, south of the ice through modern London.

When the Glaciers were actively on the move they carried in them rocks and stones from further north, which, when the ice melted, were deposited in our area. These 'erratics', as they are called, are not common but over the years have been sought after by some people. A collection of them can be seen in the Castle grounds in Hertford, also many of our old churches have large chunks built into their walls.

One of the most important results of the ice ages and subsequent melting of the caps was the laying down of beds of clay, brick-earth, gravels and

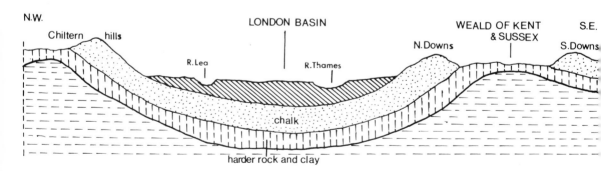

FIGURE 1.   Sketch section through the Weald–London Basin–Chilterns, showing how the chalk 'crests' of the 'waves' have eroded away to expose the underlying Greensands and Clays.

Colour Plate I. Mesolithic village at Ware, looking south across the Lea. The fishermen's boats are tethered at the riverside. The hunters are away but the domestic life goes on: cleaning and scraping skins, chopping wood for the fires, repairing fishing spears and preparing flint cores for striking off blades and scrapers.

sands, by the meltwaters outflowing from the ice. This 'drift' geology has largely determined the flora and fauna of the countryside and the consequent land usage and agriculture of south-east England.

The clays, brick-earths (a type of light, easily moulded clay) and light gravels overlie the chalk and when cultivated are highly fertile, particularly suitable for the growing of barley and similar cereals. The river valleys, with their alluvium and peat, form good pasturage and the deep moist land is suitable for grazing or nursery type cultivation. Where the sand, gravels and clays are acid and deep, the soil is less fertile but supports good and often dense growths of forest and scrub timber, as the area to the south of the Lea where the chalk is thicker and is overlain by clay with flints, acid pebbley sands of the Reading Beds and the thick blue clay of the London Basin. All this makes for a heavy, more acid environment which, nevertheless, supports an abundance of ancient woodlands – also you can grow rhododendrons south of the Lea, but not north.

Due north and north-west of the Lea, there are mainly gravels and sand, to the north-east towards Bishop's Stortford there is a large area of brick-earths and boulder clays. This drift material is overlying the chalk, which in places is exposed on the surface, particularly as one moves northward where the scars of ancient chalk pits are still features of the landscape.

The rivers of Eastern Hertfordshire flow in a general direction from north-west to south-east following the dip slope of the Chilterns. The Lea, or Lee, rising at Luton flows mainly eastward through Hertford to Ware. Just after Ware it turns due south to reach the Thames, east of London. The Lea on its way to the Thames collects all the other streams and rivers of the eastern side of the County. The tributaries of the Mimram and Beane join it at Hertford, the Rib just to the east of the town and the Ash and Stort a little further downstream to the east of Ware. The Lea, as it turned south, was therefore a fair-sized river and carved out a wide valley, particularly when it was swollen by melting ice ten thousand or so years ago. Since then the Lea Valley has largely silted up and in many areas has formed thick peat beds and rich alluvial flats in the wide river valley.

Geology determined the geography and development of this area and it determined where Hertford and Ware were going to grow. Our geology affects us in many ways. Our water, so important in the development of all agriculture and horticulture, is mainly drawn from the great chalk dip of the London Basin. The water lies in this great bowl as it is sealed in by the impervious layer of clay beneath the chalk. Our water, with the dissolved chalk in it, is some of the hardest in the country. If we pump too much water out of this bowl the water table goes down and our rivers dry up or become mere shadows of their former swift flowing selves.

The brick-earths and lighter boulder clays have always provided good clay for pot and brick making. For example, a major Roman pottery industry existed at Bromley Hall Farm, between Standon and Much Hadham, making pots and tiles. We had pottery kilns in Roman Ware making pots in a hard grey ware. In the Medieval period there were many small potteries scattered throughout our area. The railway viaducts at Welwyn and Hertford were built from bricks made locally on site. The yellow stock bricks used extensively in buildings in Ware and Hertford are made from the local clay. The brickyards at Ware (now partially covered by the western part of Glaxo) were famous for the production of unique styles of bricks invented by Caleb Hitch. Another major industry known to all is the extraction and processing of sands and gravels. Many thousands of acres of the Lea Valley itself and the lowland margins have been blighted by this all-consuming activity.

When the chalk was laid down in the still water, fifty million or so years ago, nodules of flint formed, at various levels, from the siliceous remains of millions of sea creatures. As the exposed chalk is dissolved away by the action of rain, which contains carbonic acid, the flints and clay remain. Much of our area is literally covered with flints on the surface, mostly in small pebble form but also, as at Foxholes Farm just to the south-west of Hertford, in layers of very large nodules a foot or two in diameter.

Flint has a free structure and can be struck and flaked into sharp tools such as axes, knives, arrow heads, and spear heads. Until the discovery of metals, flint along with wood and bone provided most of the tools and weapons of mankind. It also provides one of our main natural building materials. The chalk itself, which in some areas is hard enough to build with, provides us with a material locally called 'clunch', which was used extensively in the construction of churches and public buildings.

Another type of stone found in our area is that called 'pudding stone'. Regarded more as an oddity than a real building stone it is the result of certain geological processes. It occurs where the chalks, clays and gravels overlap. This conglomerate is formed under conditions of great heat and pressure, it is extremely hard and is like concrete with flint pebbles of various sizes set in the chalky matrix. It was occasionally used in buildings, but from prehistoric times onwards its main use was to make quern stones and millstones for grinding corn.

Our two towns lie close to where four rivers join the Lea; the Mimram, Beane, Ash and Rib. They are also at the junction of two distinct geological areas. The acid sands, gravels and clays lie to the south. The more fertile, lighter brick-earths, boulder clays and gravels over chalk are to the north. The sites of the two towns must have always been natural centres for their immediate hinterlands (see Fig. 4, p. 20).

HERTFORD

The geology of Hertford and the immediate neighbourhood is fairly simple. The base sediments of the river valleys formed the rich alluvium. This is particularly deep to the west of Hertford, under Hartham Common and the water meadows and meads towards Ware. This alluvium overlies the heavier gravel and the valley sides are composed of gravel terraces, which are capped in some places by boulder clay or brick-earth. The underlying basal chalk is exposed in places, for example, at Chadwell Springs on the south side of the Hertford to Ware road. It also appears at the very bottom of the rivers in places as a whitish marl.

At this point we should perhaps pause to consider the importance of the River Lea. Downstream from Hertford it has now become a relatively narrow river, flowing in a wide valley bottom. For about ten thousand years this wide valley has existed. In most places marshy, it has ever presented an obstacle to crossing by foot or horse traffic and the river itself was generally too deep to be forded easily.

The first natural ford, up the Lea from the Thames in prehistoric times, was probably at Hertford. The most likely place for this would be in the area of the present Millbridge, just below the junction of the Lea and Mimram but upstream of the Beane and the Rib. At this place the Lea and the Beane run through a narrowing in the valley between the ridge at the bottom of Port Hill, on the northern side, to the rising terrace of Queen's Road on the southern side. The distance here is only some five hundred metres. Between the Beane at Cowbridge and the Lea is a gravel ridge. This ridge runs from Sele Farm past Hertford County Hospital and continues down to meet the Lea at Old Cross. It formed and still does form a relatively elevated piece of ground between these two rivers and makes two easy crossings possible.

It is difficult to determine exactly where the original land surface started to rise to the south of the Lea. Excavations in Maidenhead Street and the Green Dragon Yard showed little sign of gravel there, only a depth of occupation debris and alluvium. But certainly the ground is rising by the time the War Memorial in Parliament Square is reached. The distance between the gravel terraces north and south of the Lea, is something like 100 to 150 metres. The distance across the valley of the Beane is well under that. This narrow gap, in fact, formed a small shelf over which the rivers ran as shallows. For a mile or more upstream the rivers would have run fairly slow and deep through low water meadows, which were probably always wet and muddy and in the winter months, impossibly marshy and difficult to cross. At Millbridge, with the change of level, the rivers ran fast over the shallows which would have had a firm gravelly bottom. Down-stream the valley broadened and became flatter as far as Ware. This change of level, slight though it was, provided two fords (one across the Lea and one across the Beane) easily reached from the higher ground to north and south, with a stepping-stone of higher ground in the middle (see Fig. 13, p. 80).

Excavations by the Hertfordshire Archaeological Trust in 1990, at Millbridge, uncovered a Roman land surface some three metres below the existing street level; about the height of the present river bed. Other excavations a bit further away from the river in St Andrew Street, showed that the ancient land level was some three metres higher there. Thus the area around Millbridge seems to offer the most natural fording place of both the Lea and the Beane.

At the close of the last ice age, some 10,000 years ago, these rivers no doubt diverged from their present course and wandered about across the valley bottom. When the snow and ice outwashed from the Glaciers the whole wide valley was probably a raging torrent. Then as the climate warmed and steadied, the rivers narrowed and cut their present courses deep into the soft alluvial debris. There is no reason to suppose that there has been any real change in the course of these two rivers over the past 5,000 years or so. Of course both rivers may well have been deeper and wider at times than they now are.

At the present time the Mimram joins the Lea near the Hertford Football Club, in the water meadows a kilometre to the west of the town. However, it may not always have run so. There is another course that this river could have taken, along the northern side of the valley and joining the Lea almost opposite the present Castle Hall which is just upstream from the suggested site of the ford. By following the line of the stream or ditch running from the Castle grounds, past the south side of St Andrews Church, its older course can still clearly be seen. We will discuss this further when we look at the evidence for the foundation of the Saxon *burghs* at Hertford.

The road plans support the position of the ford close to Millbridge. Assuming prehistoric man was using the ford from say 5,000 BC onwards then major trackways and cross-country routes would soon become established. When used over a number of generations these would tend to become fossilized as part of the landscape. If one looks at the two roads of Cowbridge and St Andrew Street their lines converge on the river some-where from the present Millbridge to about fifty metres downstream. So anywhere thereabouts is a possible site for the original fording place of the Lea. It is quite likely that the ford would have been fairly wide, consequently, the river could have been fordable in several places in this area.

WARE

The geology and geography around Ware, although generally similar to Hertford, differs in some important respects. Firstly, the sides of the valley to the south are steep and the underlying chalk is exposed as scarps in places. The valley on the other side of the Lea gently slopes up to the low gravel hills which lie to the north bordering the river valley. The southern-most part of this area north of the Lea is a mixture of fine brick-earths and pockets of soft sand. The general area encompassed by Glaxo's, Buryfields and Baldock Street was particularly favoured for early settlement. This, especially the easternmost parts, lies mainly on the river gravels, with overlays of brick-earths, sands and alluvium. It is fertile, well drained and faces due south and is sheltered by wooded hills to the north. Two small streams (the Lower and Upper Bourne) outflowed into the Lea within what was to become the grounds of the fourteenth-century Friary (the present day Priory grounds).

In ancient times the Lea at Ware was probably nearly twice the size of the river at Hertford. But there is a similar narrowing of the river valley between the chalk cliffs of Chadwell Springs Golf Club, on the south side, and the brick-earth slope on the north side of the river, on which the main Glaxo complex now stands. These two areas are only about 600 metres apart. But, unlike Hertford, the valley between these two points is deep and has no raised ridge in the centre. By the time the Lea gets to Ware two more tributaries have joined it thus much increasing the volume of the river. This suggests that, at least in the early period, a major ford at Ware was unlikely.

Until bridges were built at Ware, and other places further downstream, Hertford would have been a more natural place for crossing. Movement to and from East Anglia going north-east and south-southwest would need to pass through, or somewhere close to Hertford. Likewise, traffic proceed-ing directly north–south from the eastern side of Britain would cross at Hertford. In Roman times the main north–south traffic would of course have used the Ware bridge and the Ermine Street, thus bypassing Hertford. But when that bridge fell into disrepair, travellers may once again have reverted to the Hart ford.

Taking into account all that has been said above, it seems unlikely that Ware's early development was due to the existence of a ford, at least not a major ford. Even crossings of the river by dugout canoe or raft would have been hazardous, especially during the winter floods. But we know from the evidence recovered during extensive excavations, in the 1970s and 80s, that prehistoric settlement did begin some 8,000 years ago during the Mesolithic period. The sheltered south-facing slope looking out over the river afforded a very favourable position for early man – good drainage, ready access to the fishing in the river, plenty of good foraging for fruits and berries along the river margins. All these were prime requirements for primitive societies.

Ware's Medieval and later prominence was undoubtedly due to its position on the River Lea. Ware, probably at the upper extent of reasonable navigation on the Lea, was a natural inland port for water transport. Likewise, in late prehistoric times, it was of prime importance as the focus for entrepreneurs from the Continent seeking to trade with the pre-Roman Iron Age peoples of the hinterland, like those who lived in the large urbanized centres, or *oppida*, such as that discovered at Puckeridge. Excavations there in the early 1970s, by the Hart Archaeological Unit, recovered large quantities of pottery and metalwork, imported from the Continent. Thirty years or so later the Romans arrived. Their great north road, the Ermine Street, struck out from London and after passing through Enfield arrowed its way due north to cross the River Lea at Ware. The bridge was almost certainly originally a military venture, constructed to facilitate the rapid movement of troops and equipment. That the Ermine Street eventually stretched from London to Scotland and long stretches are still in use today, testifies to the enduring importance of this highway.

The warm and well drained south-facing river terraces, the deep-water navigation and the advantage of being on a major north–south route all contributed to the making and prospering of Ware for some 8,000 years.

2
The Background

Archaeology is the study of the material remains of mankind's past from earliest times; and even up to the present day when no literary or historical evidence is available. History is the study and chronicling of mankind's progress and achievement in written form. Our story is compiled from elements of both these disciplines, plus a liberal sprinkling of personal views and comments.

The story of mankind probably begins in Africa sometime in excess of four million years ago. The first ape-like proto-men gradually evolved and developed into 'near' men, called *Homo Erectus*. We know that they used fire and simple tools made from stone or wood. By about 100,000 years ago 'true' men had arrived in the shape of Neanderthal man and our direct ancestors *Homo Sapiens Sapiens*. Neanderthal man gradually disappeared from the scene leaving *Homo Sapiens Sapiens* to develop fully into modern man. By 10,000 years ago the last ice age was ending and the plains and tundra of northern Europe were warming up. Man now became more mobile and was able to survive away from the deep caves and rock shelters, which was the usual habitat during the colder periods. The fairly static hunters of the tundra and ice margins now became more nomadic and began to wander far afield from their former haunts; the Paleolithic (Old Stone Age) was over. With the burgeoning flora of the warmer climate, family groups and bands of foragers began to exploit the scrub forests and river margins. They became not only hunters of beasts and birds, but fishers and gatherers of berries and edible plants. This new era was called the Mesolithic, or Middle Stone Age; it lasted until approximately 3,000 BC.

During the fifth and fourth millennia BC new peoples and ideas moved up through the fertile valleys of south and central Europe, eventually penetrating into northern Europe and Britain. These groups, known as the Neolithic, or New Stone Age peoples, brought with them a new and more settled way of life. They were stock rearers and herders, farmers and agriculturalists. Their more settled way of life was in direct contrast to the earlier nomadic hunters, fishers and gatherers. With the arrival of farming we see the beginnings of deforestation that over the next 4,000 years or so was to result in the denudation of 90 per cent of our primeval forests. 'Slash and burn' methods of land clearance soon began to make inroads into the marginal forest lands bordering the lighter clays and chalklands favoured by the Neolithic farmers.

The process of deforestation continued and increased with an influx of Continental people bringing with them metal tools of copper and bronze. These Bronze Age peoples were mainly stock rearers and ranchers and needed large open tracts of countryside to run their stock on. Their much sharper bronze axes would have been at least twice as efficient as flint axes at clearing the scrub and light forest margins (Plate 1). From about 600 BC even more efficient tools, made of iron, arrived from northern Europe, thus accelerating the process.

About 150 BC the murky window of history begins to clear. Late Iron Age people, called the Belgae, lived in northern Gaul (modern France and Belgium). They were a warlike people and internecine squabbles among the tribes resulted in large family groups and warrior bands crossing the Channel to carve out territories for themselves in Britain. They settled in southeastern Britain and at last we now begin to learn something about them from ancient writers.

In 55 and 54 BC the famed Roman general, Julius Caesar, invaded Britain. His legions defeated the descendants of those first Belgic settlers but after exacting hostages and tribute the Romans returned to Gaul where other Belgic tribes were in revolt and causing trouble.

PLATE 1.   Late Bronze Age axe and sword from the Hertford area. Hertford Museum.

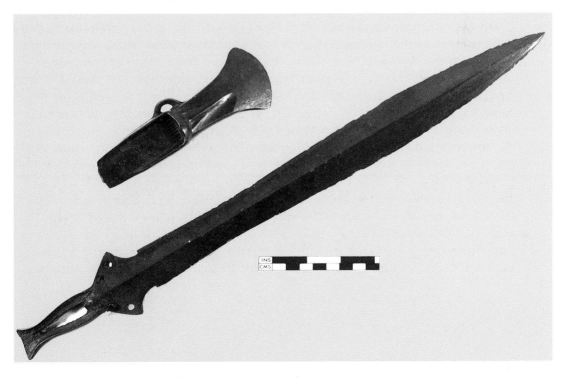

PLATE 2.   Palaeolithic hand axes (top) and a Neolithic polished stone axe. Ware Museum.

It was almost a century before the Emperor Claudius brought four legions to Britain to complete the conquest of the British tribes. This time the Romans remained here for nearly 400 years. During the fourth and fifth centuries AD bands of Saxon mercenaries arrived in Britain to aid the Britons against the raiding Picts. Later on more Saxons, Angles and Jutes began to arrive – much as the Belgae had nearly 600 years before. Over the next hundred years or so the eastern and south-eastern parts of Britain came fully under the sway of these fierce warrior-settlers. By the late sixth century the *Adventus Saxonorum* was firmly established, despite the spirited resistance of the Britons who fought many bloody battles against the Saxon hordes. The seventh century heralded the rise of the 'English' kingdoms in Kent, Essex, Mercia, Northumbria and East Anglia. At the end of the eighth century the Danes arrived, firstly as hit and run raiders, then in increasing numbers to seize land and settle. In the next hundred years they overran much of northern and eastern England and were only defeated and dispersed by King Alfred in the late ninth century. After Alfred's death in 901, his son Edward and his daughter Aethelflead carried on the fight against the Danes and by the time of Edward's death, in 924, they had recovered nearly all of England from them.

Though the power of the Danes had been irrevocably broken on land, they continued to harry and plunder from their mobile fleets of ships and this intermittent raiding continued until a Scandinavian King, Cnut, united Norway, Denmark and England under one banner over a hundred years later.

In 1066 came William of Normandy to lay dubious claim to the English throne. The events of that year are well known and need no reiteration here.

In our area we have little evidence for Old Stone Age inhabitants and what there is has come from casual finds of stone tools, mainly hand axes which were roughly chipped from flint. These flint axes varied in size from ten centimetres to about thirty. They were roughly pear-shaped, held in the hand and had a multitude of uses; for digging, chopping and smashing bone, scraping and cleaning hides and for butchering. You can see examples of them in the Hertford and Ware Museums (Plate 2).

Our story about Ware and Hertford really starts in the dim and distant past, with the first Mesolithic settlement at Ware. On present evidence Ware can lay claim to being considerably older as a settlement than Hertford, perhaps by as much as 6,000 years. This then is where our narrative must start.

THE FIRST SETTLERS AT WARE

Imagine you are standing at the lower end of Fanshawe Crescent at the junction with Park Road, with the rising ground behind you to the north. You are looking out over what is now the Glaxo complex but then was just a scrubby grass slope leading down to the river. Let's say it is an April day in *c.* 7000 BC. The weather is still fairly chill, the river valley is still flooded after the thaw of the winter snows on the Chilterns and higher ground. The valley bottom would probably be considerably lower than it is at present, with reed beds, mud banks, and isolated stretches of shallow water in places. The marshes are full of birds and the river full of fish. Behind you the slope northwards is covered in birch, alder and pine. In front of you the scrub and bushes have been cleared and there is a settlement of some eight or ten primitive huts. These are mainly semicircular or oval shaped, probably constructed of skins stretched over wicker and wooden supports and per-haps in places covered with turf or some reed thatching. Drawn up below the huts, on the river bank, are dugout canoes with osier fish traps scattered around. There may be fish spears or leisters and long poles with running loops made from thin strips of hide, used to catch large fish or fowl by dropping the loop over their unwary heads.

The people are probably dressed in made-up furs. Several fires are alight between, but away from the huts, with fish and duck cooking on spits or maybe on hot flat stones, or perhaps even in leather buckets; these would be kept boiling by dropping hot stones (pot boilers) from the embers of the fire into them. Outside one hut a man is chipping away at selected nodules of flint to make flint cores. His companion is probably using a bone punch to strike off fine flint flakes from these prepared cores; these tiny fragments of flint, called microliths, were used to construct composite tools and weapons like knives, arrows and harpoons. Elsewhere, deer hides are pegged out on racks and a woman is using a sharp flint scraper to clean the hides. You may see a hunting party of perhaps four men and two boys who are returning from the woods to the north, carrying the carcass of a deer slung from a pole (Col. Plate I, p. 3).

This might have been typical of a day in the life of the Mesolithic settlement, uncovered during excavations by the Hart Archaeological Unit under the direction of Clive Partridge in the 1970s. The excavations, in advance of the redevelopment of the old Allen & Hanbury's Sports Field, uncovered the abundant remains of a small Roman town and an underlying pre-Roman Iron Age settlement. Beneath these remains the excavators began to discover clusters of flint flakes, cores and scrapers; artefacts typical of the earlier Mesolithic period. These flints were found in a thin greyish layer (probably the remains of the original turfline) lying on top of the brick-earth which was the sub-soil beneath the Roman and Iron Age settlement. Eventually, after many weeks of very careful excavation, the remains of the Mesolithic settlement were laid bare. Pits, post-holes and curved gullies were there, all cut into the virgin brick-earth. The fill of many of these features contained waste flakes, worked flints and pot boilers. These were the material remains of that first settlement. To the layman this was just a collection of different sized and shaped holes in the ground but to the trained eye of the archaeologist they represented the remains of huts, windbreaks, drying racks, working hollows and drainage gullies (Plate 3).

Further redevelopment of the southern part of the factory site, some years later, enabled the Hertfordshire Archaeological Trust to continue the earlier work. This time it was some 150 metres from the original excavations and a bit closer to the river. Here also there was evidence of Mesolithic occupation, though more scattered and less well preserved.

From these remains it is reasonable to assume that the Mesolithic occupation was of a fairly substantial and long-lived nature. These Middle Stone Age hunters and fishers may well have lived on this site from about 7,000 BC until around 3,000 BC. Evidence for Mesolithic occupation has also been found in other places nearby. For example, at Broxbourne, Stanstead Abbotts and Cuffley. Many other settlement sites have undoubtedly been lost to us during earlier phases of gravel extraction or, indeed, may still be awaiting discovery. At Ware we appear to have something more than the usual temporary hunting camp establishment. It seems more likely to have been

PLATE 3.   Some of the Mesolithic features found during excavations at Glaxo's Ware. The
curved gullies and post-holes are the last visible remains of huts and
windbreaks.

a permanent base camp, perhaps approaching the size of a small village. So
far, no evidence for occupation of this antiquity has turned up in Hertford,
but excavations anywhere along the river margins could change this picture
at any time.

THE FARMERS ARRIVE

The next people to arrive in our area were the first Neolithic farmers,
probably around 5,000 years ago. These new people were mainly farmers
and stock rearers and during the fourth and third millennia BC began to
clear the trees and scrublands on the low chalk hills bordering the river
valley. At Foxholes Farm, where there now stands a large business park,
excavations were carried out in the 1970s and 80s by the Hart Archaeological
Unit. These excavations, the most comprehensive carried out on a gravel

pit site in Hertfordshire, produced ample evidence that this upland chalk and gravel plateaux was occupied and worked by these farmers. Banana-shaped holes or pits were discovered, sometimes as deep as a metre or more, and may have been used as wind shelters or working hollows. Many flint tools and weapons were recovered during the excavations: polished axe heads, scrapers, blades, knives and leaf-shaped arrowheads (Fig. 2). All these made from the flint which is to be found locally in the chalk. The flint, often burnt and calcified, was also crushed up and mixed with clay to produce crude pottery vessels. More recently, traces of occupation dating to this period have been found by the Hertfordshire Archaeological Trust during excavations along the line of the new Cole Green bypass.

We have no way of knowing whether the Mesolithic people were still living by the river at Ware when the farmers arrived and settled on the low hills on either side of the river valley. It could be that the two communities coexisted peacefully for many years, trading fish and fowl for mutton and cereals. It is quite possible that after an initial influx of new farming people the idea of farming was taken up by some of the more adventurous of the Mesolithic hunters and fishers. Whatever the overall situation, one result of the new stable lifestyle of the farmers would undoubtedly have been a significant increase in the population.

During the excavations at Glaxo's a few sherds of coarse pottery and some flint cores and scrapers of Bronze Age type were also recovered. This

FIGURE 2.   On left; drawings of Neolithic (leaf-shaped) and Bronze Age (tanged and barbed) arrowheads. On the right; Neolithic and Bronze Age scrapers. All from Foxholes Farm.

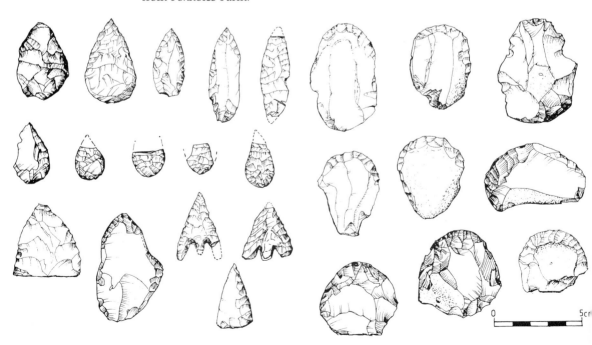

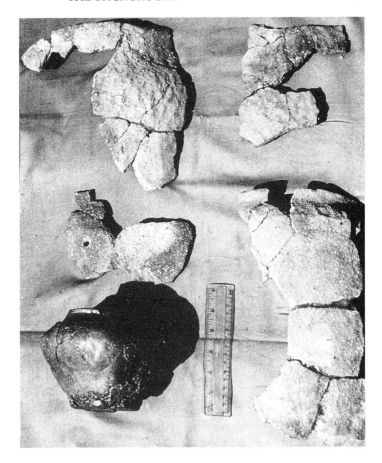

PLATE 4.   Some of the Late Bronze Age/Early Iron Age pottery recovered during
excavations at Moles Farm, Ware.

does suggest that there was at least some continuity of settlement close to
the river at Ware. However, the main Neolithic, Bronze Age and Early Iron
Age settlements were more usually sited on the higher ground. The remains
of such a settlement was discovered during the laying of a gas pipeline at
Moles Farm, a mile to the north of Ware. Robert Kiln organized a rescue
team and pits, ditches and gullies were identified and sampled. These
yielded Late Bronze Age or Early Iron Age pottery, pot boilers and many
butchered animal bones; debris from a settlement, probably a small farming
community, dating to about 600 BC (Plate 4).

South of Hertford and Ware, on the low hills around Foxholes Farm, the
picture is one of increasing activity from the late Neolithic onwards. With
the advent of the Bronze Age there was a further upsurge in the population.

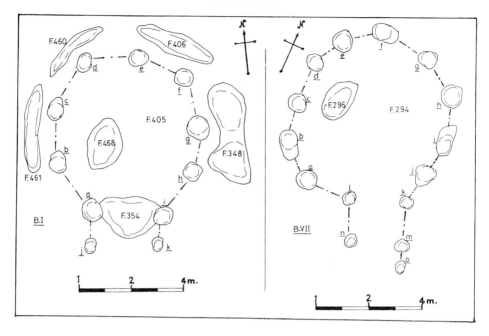

FIGURE 3.   Drawn plans of portalled round houses of Late Bronze Age date from Foxholes
Farm.

There is evidence for more widespread land usage and the construction of portalled round huts, typical of the period (Fig. 3 & Plate 5). The excavations there in the 1970s and early 80s uncovered many pits, ditches, gullies and post-hole features of this period. Several cremation burials, contained in urns, allow us some insight into burial ritual at the time (Plate 6). In one area, on the brow of the hill overlooking the river valley (just to the south

PLATE 5.   Bronze Age round house at Foxholes Farm. The thick black lines indicate the
circle of post-holes and the entranceway.

PLATE 6.   A Bronze Age cremation burial at Foxholes Farm. Heavy earth moving machines have crushed the collared urn.

of Pinehurst Estate, where a Bronze Age barrow is still preserved), a concentration of large shaft-like pits were found. These belong to the same general phase of occupation. Their form and disposition suggests that they may have had some sort of ceremonial use.

All in all it can be seen that on these low hills, overlooking the river valley, there were scenes of considerable activity in the late prehistoric period (Fig. 4). These mainly agrarian activities, which included the growing of crops and cereals, ranching and animal husbandry seem to have continued almost unchanged through the Bronze Age and into the Early Iron Age. During the Middle Iron Age a small village or farming community was established overlapping the area where had been the earlier Bronze Age shaft pits. Although the evidence for circular huts, pits and ditches was clear enough, the relatively limited amount of material remains from this period suggests a fairly short span of occupation.

In the Late Iron Age the Foxholes area was the focus for a new influx of farmer-settlers, dating possibly from about 50 BC. The major visible remains of this period was a large rectilinear, ditched enclosure. It was subdivided internally into habitation and stock pen areas. The surrounding ditch was some 1.5 metres deep with a high internal bank. From the large amount of animal bones, pottery, thatch and loom weights, metal objects and general

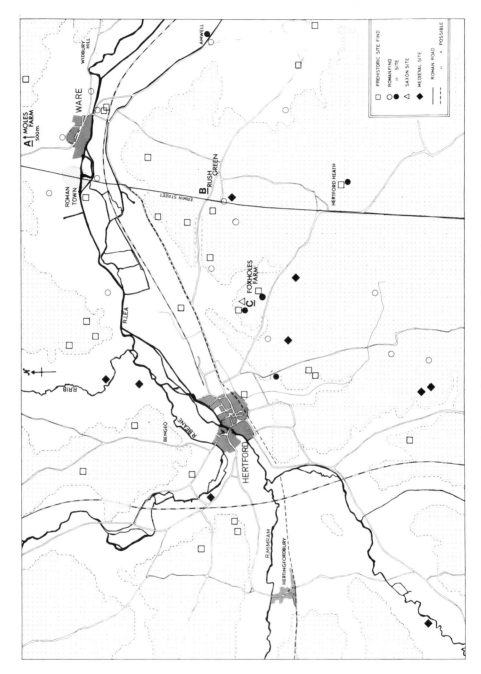

FIGURE 4.   Location map of the Hertford–Ware area, showing the rivers and valleys; the
higher ground is stippled. Sites and finds of Prehistoric to Medieval date. Note
the prominent clustering of sites belonging to the Prehistoric and Roman
periods on the higher ground.

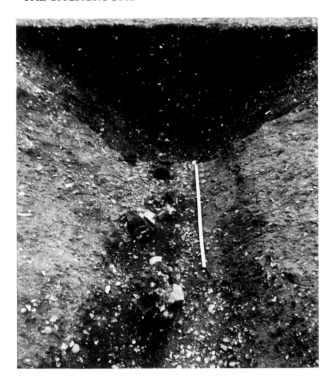

PLATE 7.   Section of the Late Iron Age enclosure ditch at Foxholes Farm. The dark stains
            indicate the position of cooking fires; broken pottery is scattered along the
            bottom of the ditch.

rubbish, recovered from the ditch it would appear that it had been used as
a general dump. Cooking fires and metal working hearths were regularly
built in the ditch, to judge from the spread of burnt material and the heavily
fired patches of clay found on the original ditch bottom (Plates 7 & 8).

This site is unusual in Hertfordshire in that no examples of imported
Gallo-Belgic pottery were found, nor any Iron Age coins. All the classic sites
of the late pre-Roman Iron Age such as those at Puckeridge, Welwyn, and
St Albans, have all produced quantities of these artefacts. Therefore, it is
almost certain that the Foxholes occupation pre-dates the major settlement
period and may relate to the movement of Late Iron Age peoples relocating
from their homelands in northern Europe. These peoples could have sailed
up by way of the Lea and spotted the advantages of the elevated site at
Foxholes. The archaic nature of the pottery and the similarly early collection
of mainly Continental brooch types leads the excavator (Clive Partridge)
and other experts on this period, to postulate more affinity with earlier Late
Iron Age sites in Kent and possibly on the Continent, than the classic

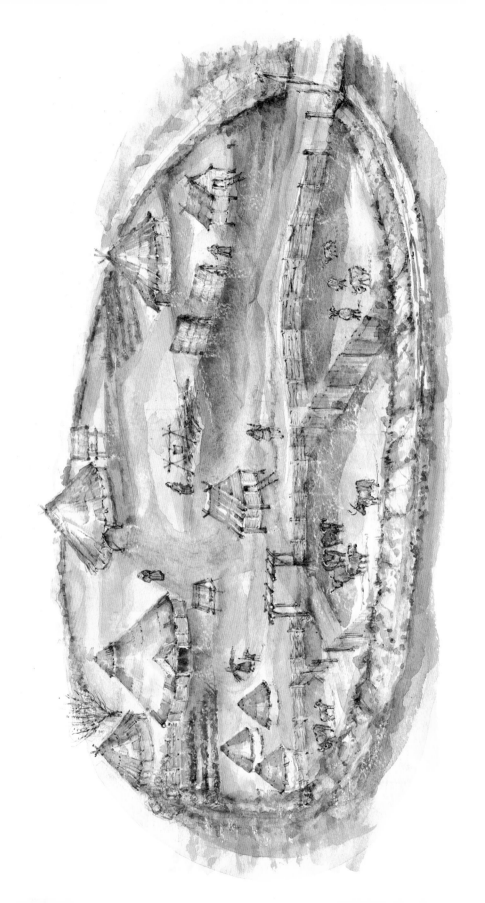

COLOUR PLATE II.   An Iron Age settlement at Foxholes Farm, Hertford. The ditched an banked enclosure surrounds the domestic huts and cattle pens. The scene is one of considerable activity.

PLATE 8.   Part of the Late Iron Age enclosure at Foxholes Farm during the excavations in
             1977.

Hertfordshire and Essex sites. Had the occupation been later in date, or
lasted for a longer period of time, the more usual pottery types, brooches,
imported pottery and coins would all have been present (see Col. Plate II).

While all this has been going on a mile or so away, Hertford appears to
have remained unoccupied, just a low ridge of gravel in the marshy river
valley. At least nothing has as yet been discovered around the ford or in
the town centre to indicate any early settlement in the valley or use of the
ford. Of course, one should realize that any such early material may be
buried deep beneath the debris of 2,000 years of occupation. This lack of
present evidence does not preclude the possibility that ancient man did
make use of the natural fording place, for crossing to and from the higher
land on either side of the river.

THE EMERGENCE OF BRITAIN INTO THE HISTORICAL RECORD

With the expeditions of Julius Caesar, in 55 and 54 BC, come the first written
references to the tribes and war leaders in Southern Britain. Caesar was not

only an able administrator and general but he kept extensive notes of his campaigns in Gaul and Britain, which he eventually wrote down in his *De Bello Gallico*. We know that he landed somewhere along the south coast and proceeded to scatter the forces of the British tribes. He crossed the Thames and headed towards Colchester where the leaders of the Trinovantes concluded a treaty. From Colchester Caesar penetrated into the territory of Cassivellaunus, one of the most powerful of the British tribal chieftains. Caesar's legions defeated him somewhere in what is now present day Hertfordshire at his capital, which has been variously placed at Wheathamstead, Ravensburgh Castle and Puckeridge. Having exacted tribute and hostages Caesar withdrew to Gaul. After the Caesaerean campaigns Cassivellaunus disappears from the written record, to be replaced at the tribal centres which grew up at St Albans, Welwyn and Puckeridge, by other powerful but more pro-Roman leaders.

In the period between, say, 30 BC and the Claudian Conquest in AD 43, our area was part of the territory of the Catuvellauni. Their early capital was at Prae Wood just outside modern St Albans. We know the name of the leader of the Catuvellauni from the many coins minted between about 20 BC and AD 10 which carry the name of Tasciovanus, or as it is shortened on the coins, TASC or TASCI.

He in turn was succeeded by perhaps the most famous British King of the period, Cunobelinus (Shakespeare's 'Cymbeline King of the Britons'). Cunobelinus claimed to be the son of Tasciovanus and from about AD 10 he takes over the territories of Tasciovanus and from his own tribal capital at Puckeridge sets out to subjugate the Trinovantes of Essex where he eventually set up his new capital.

During this period the Catuvellauni under these two kings became the most powerful force in Southern Britain, extending their sway over most of the south-east up to Norfolk and the Midlands. Cunobelinus died in the years just before the Claudian Conquest. Indeed, his death almost certainly prompted the Roman invasion. While pro-Roman Cunobelinus was alive the Romans were happy to leave Britain well alone as a friendly trading partner. But on the death of the old King his two warlike sons, Caractacus and Togodumnus, began stirring up trouble for the Romans among the other tribes of Southern Britain. The Claudian campaign in AD 43 was the answer to this warmongering.

We are fortunate in that our knowledge of the late pre-Roman Iron Age in Hertfordshire has, in recent years, been greatly expanded by the work carried out at a number of major settlements. Of course the work of Wheeler and Frere, at Verulamium, had shown the comparative sophistication of the Late Iron Age settlement there. But other centres have come to light. For example, work in the 1970s, directed by Dr Ian Stead for the Department of the Environment, and more recently by Gil Burleigh for the North Hertford-shire Museums Service has shown Baldock to have been an important settlement in the years leading up to the Roman Conquest. Closer to home excavations and field work by the Hart Archaeological Unit, under the direction of Clive Partridge, has firmly established the existence of a major Late Iron Age settlement in the Puckeridge–Braughing area. Many hundreds of Iron Age coins have been found, along with the debris of material from their minting. Large quantities of imported pottery and artefacts are also among the assemblages. It seems quite likely that the Puckeridge settlement was equally as extensive and important as that at Prae Wood. The Pucker-idge site is revealed as one of the largest and most important Late Iron Age settlements in Southern Britain, dating from about 20 BC to AD 45. Material recovered during the excavations reveals a substantial trade with Roman Gaul, the Rhineland, Italy and Spain. We can now see that a Late Iron Age settlement discovered at Ware may well have been the port for foreign traders arriving by water, before setting off into the hinterland to trade their goods. Excavations in various parts of the town at Ware have now revealed quite extensive areas of Late Iron Age occupation on the north bank of the Lea (Fig. 5). Late Iron Age material extends from at least as far west as Ware Lock, covering the area now occupied by the Glaxo complex, Buryfields and extending to the east as far as West Street in the centre of the present town. There can be little doubt that Ware was important as a Late Iron Age settlement and its position, at probably the highest easily navigable part of the Lea, strongly suggests that it functioned as a trans-shipping port for luxury goods coming in, with possibly corn and agricultural products going out. The river in those days was probably wide and deep enough to allow trading boats from the Continent to sail, or be towed, up the Thames and Lea to dock at Ware. From there it is a short land journey north to the major settlement at Puckeridge. Or the movement of goods could have been by smaller shallow draught boats, up the Rib, Beane and possibly the Mimram, to service the smaller settlements and communities of the hinterland.

One should remember that the Lea was a tidal river as far upstream as Waltham at least. Although the tides did not reach Ware the effect of those tides would have backed up the river for some distance, allowing passage for quite deep draught vessels at least twice a day. Much work is still needed to establish the size and importance of this Iron Age port.

The overall extensive pattern of settlement and the amount of imported material suggests that our part of Hertfordshire was probably peaceful and well ordered, with farming communities and prosperous urbanized settlements. There is a notable lack of sites in the wooded areas to the south of the river Lea where the geology is composed of the heavier clays. It seems that the most preferred areas were on the gravels, brick-earths and

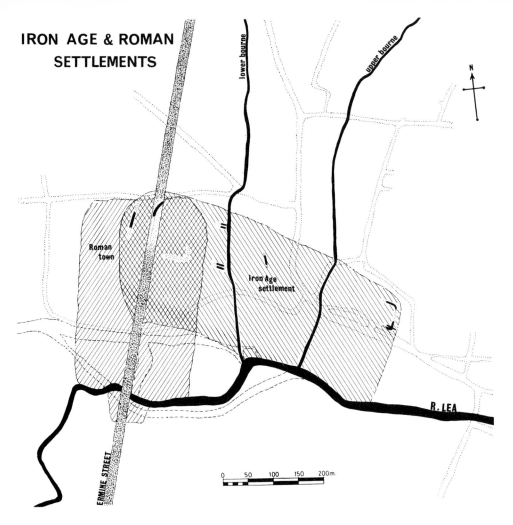

IRON AGE & ROMAN SETTLEMENTS

lower bourne

upper bourne

N

Roman town

Iron Age settlement

R. LEA

ERMINE STREET

0   50   100   150   200m.

FIGURE 5.   Plan showing the relative position of the Late Iron Age settlement and the Roman town at Ware.

the chalk hills north of the Lea and in the tributary river valleys.

Apart from the evidence for widespread nucleated occupation in our area, over the years a number of remarkably rich burials have been found, known as 'Welwyn' type burials (so called because it was at Welwyn they were first found and recognized). The burials are usually in large rectangular pits and are furnished with such things as iron fire dogs, silver cups and larger dishes, Roman amphorae (large pottery containers for carrying wine, fish sauce, or oil) and numerous other pottery vessels. These burials are very distinctive and appear to be limited to the heartland of the Catuvellauni between St Albans, Welwyn, Baldock and Puckeridge. The nearest to us is the Chieftain Burial discovered at Hertford Heath during the construction of a housing estate after the Second World War. These graves are generally assumed to be those of princes or important nobility.

We can now turn to what evidence we have for the earliest activity by the ford at Hertford. The Hertfordshire Archaeological Trust carried out excavations on the north side of the river at two sites. At No. 56 St Andrew Street, excavation produced a small quantity of pottery belonging to the late pre-Roman Iron Age or early Roman period. At Millbridge the excavators discovered a Late Iron Age or very early Romano-British burial. It was a cremation burial with the ashes in a pottery urn; a black pottery plate in imitation of a Gallo-Belgic terra nigra platter and a biconical beaker accompanied the urn (Plate 9). The burial probably took place sometime between AD 40-50. A small curved ditch was also located but was not necessarily associated with the burial. It may have been a separate enclosure or a drainage ditch surrounding a building of some sort, or it could have been a small cattle pen, or pound. This ditch appears to be slightly later than the burial and may fall more securely into the early Roman period.

These discoveries turn back the pages of Hertford's previously known history by almost 1,000 years, and surely indicate some pre-Roman or early Romano-British activity in the Millbridge and St Andrew Street area nearly 2,000 years ago. However, it has to be said that at Hertford the settlement was very much in a minor key, compared to Ware.

PLATE 9.   A Late Iron Age/Romano-British cremation group from Millbridge, Hertford.

3
The Roman Period

We have already seen from the preceding chapter that in the late pre-Roman Iron Age the major urban settlement in our area was at Puckeridge. We can say with some confidence that there was probably a port and a fair-sized riverside settlement at Ware, but any activity close to the river at Hertford was probably minimal.

In AD 41 Cunobelinus had died and his kingdom fell to two of his sons, Caractacus and Togodumnus. A third son Adminius had already fled to exile in Rome because of the internal quarrelling. During the reign of Cunobelinus the Catuvellauni had gradually conquered or taken over most of south-eastern Britain. The chiefs of other tribes had been ousted and a number of them had also fled to Roman Gaul and even to Rome itself.

Claudius, who was Emperor at the time of Cunobelinus' death, was keen to extend the Roman Empire and for many years Roman or Gaulish-Roman traders, and possibly advisers, had lived in Britain and they were probably well aware of the unpopularity of the Catuvellaunian expansion. With the death of Cunobelinus Claudius obviously saw an opportunity to rectify the situation and this prompted the invasion of Britain in AD 43. It was to be a major campaign and four full legions and a large contingent of auxiliaries, some 40,000 men, were despatched to Britain, where they eventually landed near Richborough in Kent.

Caractacus tried to defend the crossing of the Medway against the legions but his forces were defeated and scattered. The Roman army then proceeded to effect a crossing of the Thames, probably close to present-day London and marched on Colchester, which then was the capital of the Catuvellauni. It soon fell and the Romans rapidly occupied most of south-eastern Britain; as far north as Lincoln and west as far as the line of what was to become the Fosse Way, from Lincoln to Somerset. Caractacus fled north-west to the Welsh borders to try and rally support among the tribes in Wales. Meanwhile the Roman general, Vespasian, pushed on westward through Dorset, Wiltshire and into Devon meeting little or light resistance except at Maiden Castle (Fig. 6). There the Durotriges, secure inside the heavily fortified hillfort, put up a terrific fight before finally being overcome by the superior firepower and organisation of the Roman legions.

Our area being leaderless probably fell to the Romans without too much of a struggle. A burial found recently at Verulamium, dating to about AD 50, was of 'Royal' type and it may be of Adminius, the third son of Cunobelinus. He could well have been reinstated by the Romans as Chief of the Catuvellauni and his seat of power may have been at St Albans. Colchester, the former tribal capital, was made an Imperial Colonia by the Romans.

FIGURE 6.   Early military Roman roads in Southern Britain. The roads all radiate out from London and illustrate the main thrust of military campaigns in the early years.

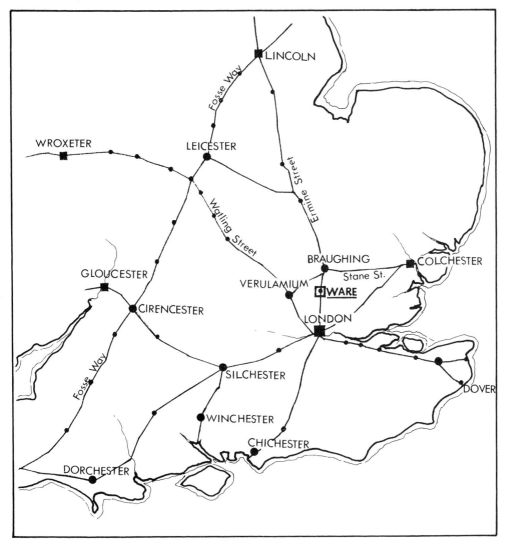

THE ROMAN TOWN AT WARE

Wherever they went one of the first things the Roman army did was build roads, a military necessity for the speedy movement of their troops. London became established as their main port of entry and Roman roads radiated out from it. Many of these roads still remain as arterial highways today. One of the most important was the route from London to Lincoln. Ermine Street, after leaving London, headed due north through Enfield and crossed the Lea at Ware. It diverted north-east to Puckeridge and then north again to Lincoln and, later on, all the way to York. The ford at Hertford, which may have seemed a more natural crossing point, was ignored. This lends credence to the suggestion that by the time the Romans arrived Ware already was established as a settlement and river port of some importance.

At Ware the Roman road approaches the river from the low chalk hills on the south side of the river valley, across what is now Chadwell Springs golf course. It crossed the valley bottom on a raised causeway to a bridge, which was sited just to the east of the present Navigation Lock. Then on northwards, through the Glaxo site and bearing a little east to take the line of what is now the A10 to Puckeridge. Though the Roman engineers were responsible for the laying out of roads, causeways and bridge works, there is little doubt that the local inhabitants would have been put to work on the labouring jobs. It can be assumed that once the road and bridge were fully operational the ford at Hertford would have been of even less importance. Ware, on the other hand, began to flourish, possibly at first as a posting station for the legions and the Imperial Mail travelling the north road. Later on the Roman civil town grew up on either side of Ermine Street, mainly on the north side of the river occupying a goodly part of what we now call the Glaxo site. There was also some development on the south bank of the river close to the southern end of the bridge.

The position of the Roman bridge can easily be pinpointed. The Roman causeway carrying the road can clearly be seen as a long, low mound crossing the valley right up to the bank of the Navigation, which is today regarded as the main river (Plate 10). After excavations by Hertford Museum in 1974, in advance of the flood relief scheme, there was revealed, close to the present course of the river, a section of the Roman Ermine Street. It was about 6 metres wide at that point and about 1 metre thick. The road was constructed from layers of gravel lying on a raised causeway made from brushwood with a chalk capping. On the west side of the road they uncovered the remains of a small rectangular building. This had been rebuilt at least once. The ground plan of the main building was roughly 4 metres

PLATE 10. Ermine Street crossing Broadmeads at Ware. The low, broad agger runs away towards the houses in the background. The people on the left are standing on the line of the eastern road ditch.

by 3 metres and it oversailed the road ditch and abutted onto Ermine Street itself, very much as though it was a check point or a toll house at the south end of the Roman bridge. This impression was reinforced by the large number of small value Roman coins found scattered on the chalk floor of the building. The excavators found traces of a boarded wooden floor and the small coins must have fallen through the cracks. The building was constructed on a substantial basal raft of chalk, to raise it above the damp, peaty alluvium (Plates 11 & 12). It is not certain when it was first constructed but we know from the coins found scattered about that it must have been in use up until AD 400, or even beyond. There are no other known examples of toll houses in Roman Britain so could the building have been something else? A small temple perhaps dedicated to the goddess or god of the River Lea?. A shrine to the Celtic god Lug may be a possibility with wayfarers leaving some small token of their thanks for a safe crossing of the river.

Before we leave the subject of Ermine Street it is worth just stressing its importance as a major highway. In Roman times it became the premier route to the north and north-east via the east Midlands, Lincoln, York, the Roman Wall and Scotland, a route which has endured largely unaltered till the present day. In our area the road has been examined in several places: Enfield, Hertford Heath, Rush Green, across the causeway in the valley south of Ware, close to the river crossing, beneath the present premises of Glaxo and in several places at Puckeridge. At Glaxo's and again at Pucker-idge there were substantial drainage ditches on either side of the road. At

PLATE 11. Excavation in progress on the rectangular building next to Ermine Street on the
south side of the river in 1974. The long scar running from right bottom to the top
of the picture is a modern Electricity Board trench.

Rush Green, which is on well-drained gravel soil, no ditches were found
but there the gravel road surface was substantial and had been repaired
and extended to a total width of some 12 metres. On its west side was a
sandy section 1.5 metres wide for the use of horses and pedestrians. Roman
horses were not often shod with iron horseshoes and a flint or gravel surface
would have been pretty devastating on their unprotected hooves. Another
interesting feature of the excavations at Rush Green was the discovery of a
number of stake or post-holes on the same alignment but beneath the road
metalling. These may have been to do with the Roman surveyors when they
were laying out the road. All the sections across Ermine Street show that it
was everywhere a substantial road, varying from 6 to 12 metres wide and
to over a metre thick. This was usually constructed with a raised central

PLATE 12. View of the chalk platform after excavation. Note how it rides over the western
road ditch and encroaches onto Ermine Street, which is on the right-hand side
of the photograph.

PLATE 13. Flood relief scheme construction near Ware Lock reveals one of the chalk rafts – damaged by the steel casement. At the top the old Allen & Hanbury buildings can be seen.

'agger' some few metres wide, with roughly level verges of sandier material for horses or pedestrians. There is usually good evidence for repair and upkeep, as would be expected for a highway as important as the Ermine Street.

The building discovered in 1974, on the south side of the river, was not alone. Remains of other chalk platforms were found in 1976 during emergency excavations, when the flood relief scheme was started on the south side close to Ware Lock. The main structural features found were the chalk rafts laid directly on the underlying peat (Plate 13). The chalk was reinforced in places by substantial gravel spreads. The rafts were some 25 cm thick and most bore traces of timber beam slots and post-holes indicating that they had supported some type of wooden building. Other clusters of thicker wooden posts and piles, found a short distance from the chalk rafts, were interpreted as part of a wharf, a landing stage, or some similar waterside structure of the Roman period.

There were many finds from these excavations and these included coarse-ware cooking pots, fine red samian wares, animal bones, waste from iron-working, an ox goad and, most exciting of all, an iron leg shackle, or slave chain (Plate 14). Whether this is evidence for the employment of slaves, or

PLATE 14. An iron slave shackle found during excavation near Ware Lock. Ware Museum.

traffic in slaves coming to Ware as 'trade' goods from abroad, is not clear but widespread use of and trade in slaves in the Roman Empire is attested by many ancient writers. Earlier finds, made when the old lock was reconstructed in 1831, include human burials, a bronze steelyard, a candlestick, an axehead, an iron ring, two puddingstone querns and a number of coins. The date of the pottery and coins from south of the river ranges from the first through to the end of the fourth century AD, though the structural evidence seems to be of mainly third and fourth century date. The occupation here may well have been associated with aspects of river transport and possibly industrial activity.

On the north side of the river the picture is more complex. Excavations between 1976 and 1984, by The Hart Archaeological Unit, were responsible for establishing the presence of a small Roman town, hitherto hidden beneath the turf and buildings of the old Allen & Hanbury sportsfield and factory (now Glaxo UK) (Plate 15). The town proper is restricted to a reasonably circumscribed area between the present millstream, on the south, and Park Road to the north. The built-up area appears not to have extended very far to the west of Ermine Street but the town may well have been more extensive on the eastern side. Any parts of the town extending into this eastern area will hopefully be preserved beneath the clubroom, changing rooms and pitch of Ware Football Club. Should the proposed move of the

PLATE 15. An aerial view of Allen & Hanbury's in 1950 (looking north). This photograph is taken, with the kind permission of Glaxo UK, from the Allen & Hanbury publication *Through A City Gateway*. It shows the factory complex as it was with the old sportsfield to the north.

club to new premises at Wodson Park come to fruition a major investigation must be a top priority, before any redevelopment of the old site, as, of course, with any further redevelopment of Glaxo's central area. In 1987 The Hertfordshire Archaeological Trust, carrying on the work of The Hart Unit, investigated the site of a proposed new development in the south-west sector of the Priory Street site. These excavations, some 100 metres west of Ermine Street, where the new Glaxo buildings S1 and S2 now stand (see Fig. 7), revealed little in the way of structural evidence. A scatter of pottery, a few coins and several scrappy inhumation burials were recovered. This is in stark contrast to the abundance of structural and artefactual evidence recovered from the areas closer to Ermine Street.

On the east side of Ermine Street there has been little opportunity for archaeological investigation beyond the Glaxo boundary. The one exception was on the very far side of the Buryfield where in 1977 a new sewer was laid right down the edge of the field. Examination of the work in progress revealed a scatter of Late Iron Age and Roman pottery, several shallow Late Iron Age ditches and a few early Romano-British burials. Further east still, behind 13-23 Baldock Street, excavations revealed a few rubbish pits and ditches containing late Roman pottery and coins. Other late Roman features, pottery and coins, were recorded in 1977 and 1981 during investigations on the site of the new extension to Ware Library and also during excavations at No. 3 West Street. In addition there have been a number of casual finds of pottery and coins in other parts of the Medieval town. This may be evidence for some late resurgence of Romano-British activity along the gravel terrace which was destined to become the site of Medieval Ware.

From our work at Glaxo's we have been able to build up a fairly coherent picture of the Roman town. We can now make some educated guesses at the overall extent of the occupation. Parts of several cemeteries have been located and in other areas scattered burials mark the outer edges of the town. Roman law was very strict about disposal of the dead. No one was allowed to be buried within the town limits. Exceptions to this were so called 'baby burials'. These were stillborn, short term or post-birth fatalities. Some of these were deliberate, because in working communities girl babies in excess were often unwelcome and were 'exposed' to get rid of them. They are quite commonly found on Roman sites, where the tiny skeletons are often buried beneath the floors of houses, or close by outside (Plate 16).

FIGURE 7.   Plan of the present day Glaxo complex (courtesy of Glaxo Operations UK). The sites and dates where Roman burials were discovered and the line of the Ermine Street are marked.

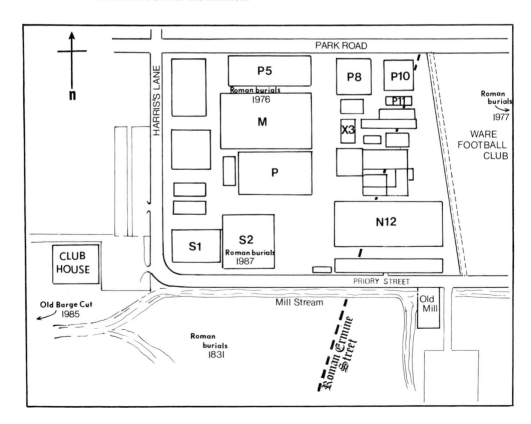

PLATE 16. The skeleton of a Romano-British baby discovered at Glaxo's in 1978. Note the out of proportion size of the skull to the tiny bones of the spine, hands and legs.

So having located at least some of the cemeteries, we can now begin to trace the outer limits of the town proper.

The first cemetery, discovered in 1976 on the north-western part of the old sportsfield, almost led to a National Emergency! We had been informed that a JCB driver reported hitting something solid during trenching for drains. Investigation soon revealed that the object was a solid lead liner from a Roman coffin. The JCB driver had been injudicious enough to mention to some watching Allen & Hanbury staff that a 'grave' had been found. Someone immediately phoned the police with some garbled message about bodies being found. We had only been working for about fifteen minutes when all hell seemed to break loose – police sirens were screeching in from several different directions to converge on the Park Road area. We were soon surrounded by a dozen policemen, ranging from a young recruit to at least a Chief Superintendent. We weren't exactly handcuffed and thrown into the black maria, that had also turned up, but it did take a bit of fast talking to convince the police that we were bona fide archaeologists. Even so we were ordered to down tools for several hours until the Coroner could be contacted. An on-site inquiry was conducted to establish the age of the burial. When the Coroner was satisfied that the burial was probably more than 100 years old he lost interest and we were allowed to carry on with our work. Meanwhile, the patently disappointed policemen gradually drifted away, no doubt to reflect on the prospect of instant promotion being wrested from their grasp.

The burial in the lead-lined coffin was carefully excavated round and by using wooden spars and rope slings we were able to lift it intact, and with the help of Allen & Hanbury's Motor Transport department were able to transfer the whole package to Hertford Museum Annexe. Work on it there revealed inside the liner a skeleton of a male, about forty at the time of death (Plates 17 & 18). A total of six inhumations were eventually recovered from this area. All of them were originally in wooden coffins, as the brownish stains in the brick-earth revealed, and the large iron nails originally holding the coffins together were found. Two of them had heavy lead liners as the first one did. This is usually the sign of a fairly important person, because even in Roman times lead was not a cheap commodity. It is also usually the sign of a Christian burial, where pains were taken to preserve the body for resurrection day. The Christian aspect was further confirmed by the east-west orientation of the graves.

On the other hand, the burials discovered on the east side of the Buryfield were pagan cremations, with the burnt ashes interred in a pottery urn. The associated pottery and material tell us that these were mainly first or second century burials.

We therefore have the location of two cemeteries, one to the east and one to the west of the town. The rather scrappy burials found in 1987, to the south-west, were also inhumations but were not nearly as carefully interred as those from Cemetery I. It could be that here we are looking at the 'poor-man's' cemetery in contrast to the 'rich-man's' cemetery to the north-west;

PLATE 17.   Lead coffin liner found in 1976 at Glaxo's. It has been cleared ready for lifting to Hertford Museum.

COLOUR PLATE III.   A view of the Roman town at Ware, looking south towards Londinium.
It has been reconstructed from elements of buildings found during
excavations with a liberal dash of artistic licence (drawn from elements
of site plans and photographs by Clive Partridge and coloured by
Joy Norris).

PLATE 18. At Hertford Museum the contents of the lead liner were carefully cleaned out to reveal the skeleton of a Romano-British male about 40 years old.

this is not an unusual arrangement and Roman cemeteries are often found with enclosures or areas set aside for richer burials; presumably those for families of substance able to afford private plots – much as the family vaults of Victorian days.

The position of the cemeteries can indicate where the town limits end but they do not tell us precisely where the town itself was. But at least, if we take the closest limits of where burials have been found, we do have a reasonably enclosed area bounded by the river to the south, Park Lane to the north, Cemetery I to the west and Cemetery II on the east side of the Buryfield (see Fig. 7, p. 36).

Occupational History of Roman Ware

A rolling programme of redevelopment, pursued firstly by Allen & Hanbury and in later years by Glaxo UK, has enabled the archaeologists to examine various parts of the 'town' often in considerable detail. The remains discovered have proved to be substantial and complex as befits an occupation that spanned at least 400 years.

The earliest specifically Roman feature found on the site was the 'Military Way', a road built by the Roman army in the opening years of the conquest to provide speedy access to the north during the first year or two of the campaigns. This has been examined in two places under Glaxo's. At the northern end of the town close to Park Road, where major excavations took place from 1976-9 (in the area now occupied by buildings P8 and P10), it was only partly overlain by the later civil road – Ermine Street (Plate 19). In 1984-5 when some of the old pastille buildings were cleared to make way for a new warehouse (N12 on the plan, Fig. 7, p. 36) the Military Way was seen again. Here the Ermine Street had been laid directly on top of the military road, completely covering it. Although this military road was only some six metres wide it was remarkably well constructed. The thickness of the road was not great (considerably less than a foot in some places) but it had a base layer of crushed chalk and sandy gravel, hard rammed to an almost concrete-like consistency. On top of this selected medium-sized cobbles had been set and rammed in. It is a good example of high quality roadmaking, showing astute appreciation of locally available materials by the army engineers. The replacement for the military road – Ermine Street – was not nearly as well constructed. Although it was up to four times thicker than the early road the metalling of Ermine Street was much more varied and loosely packed. The cambered 'agger' of the road was made up of interleaved layers of sand, gravel and some chalk. The unconsolidated

PLATE 19. The western ditch of the Military Way is closest to the ranging rod. The later ditch of the civil Ermine Street is to the right. In the section beyond the ditches many layers of chalk, clay and gravel illustrate how buildings were superimposed one on another; eventually covering the ditches and encroaching significantly onto the surface of Ermine Street.

nature of this road surface had obviously not worn too well; much patching and remaking of potholes and ruts was evident where the road was examined (see Plate 24, p. 45). The only other features that can be ascribed to the earliest phase of occupation are a couple of short lengths of ditches with the typical straight-sided, 'ankle-breaker' military profile. Finds from these earliest times are restricted to a couple of coins of the Emperor Claudius, some early South Gaulish samian pottery, and a few pieces of bronzework from military trappings. There is no doubt that the initial settlement would have been of a military nature, probably a garrison of mixed cavalry and auxilia (non-legionary soldiers) to guard the river crossing against any marauding bands of natives. Ware, being about twenty miles north of the main Roman base at Londinium, was about the right distance for a staging point on the Imperial Mail route to the north. Imagine the scene . . . a sweating, near exhausted, horse and rider approaching from the south carrying important dispatches for the General commanding the legions on the northern campaigns. A clatter of hooves on the bridge . . . much shouting and possibly trumpet blowing from the guards to alert the garrison of the arrival, a fresh horse and rider standing by for the transfer of the Mail, then off at a gallop to the next stopover some twenty miles or so further north. The incoming messenger and his exhausted horse fed, watered and bedded down to await any return messages from the north. One can imagine that it operated very much on the same principle as the American Pony Express in the old Wild West.

The presence of a military post would have attracted many other, non-military people. Traders, artisans and general hangers-on would be drawn here. Later on inns and lodging houses may have sprung up at this, the first river crossing of the major northbound route. When the military finally moved on the town would have continued to flourish and then grow in its own right.

Unfortunately we know relatively little about the early life of the town. The areas where most of the evidence probably lies have not yet become available for investigation. Those areas are still covered by buildings erected in the later 1940s and 50s (when a large number of Roman artefacts were collected during this construction work: and it was also rumoured that part of a tesselated Roman pavement was seen, though we have not been able to confirm this). However, our work on the more peripheral parts of the site have provided us with abundant evidence for the state of the town in the third and fourth centuries. In company with many other small Roman towns in Britain, the archaeology reveals a picture of neglect and possible abandonment of certain parts of the town in the later second and third centuries. An exception to this is the evidence for at least one family of potters, still working in the town during the latter part of the second century

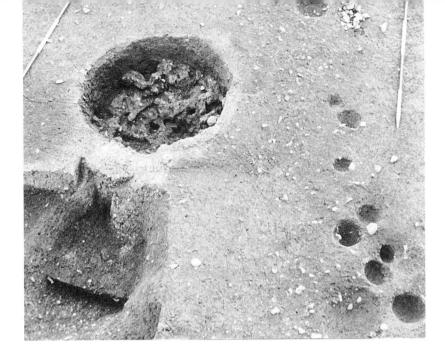

PLATE 20. Roman pottery kiln at Glaxo's. The line of post-holes with the gap in the middle may have been a fence with a gate for access to the kiln from the workshop.

and possibly into the third. The remains of a pottery kiln were discovered in an area some 60 metres back from the Ermine Street (see Plates 20 & 21). Several deep pits were found, from which the brick-earth clay had been

PLATE 21. In this photograph the kiln and some of the claypits can be seen. South of the kiln a fourth-century skeleton of a young female can be seen (dubbed 'Ermintrude' by the diggers).

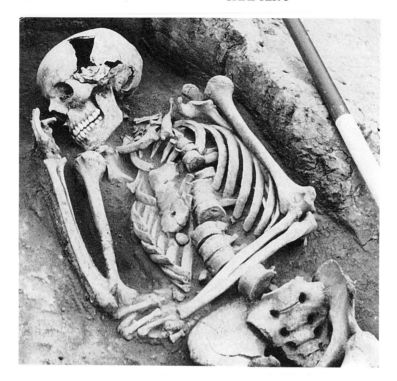

PLATE 22. 'Ermintrude' had an excellent set of teeth at the time of her death. The teeth
              are a good guide to her relative youth. From the mid-20s teeth of Romano-
              British people became increasingly worn down by the abrasive grit in the stone
              ground flour and meal that formed a large part of their diet.

dug to make the pug for pot making. The kiln was producing a fairly
distinctive type of greyware pottery (dubbed by the archaeologists 'Ware'
ware). Much waste material and broken pottery was recovered from the
stokehole and firing chamber of the kiln; also from a variety of other features
such as pits and ditches. A stray inhumation burial was discovered here
(Plates 21 & 22). There was graphic evidence close by the kiln for fences
and light post-hole structures, which may have been part of the potters'
workshop (Plate 23).

   Then once more there is abundant evidence for a resurgence in the for-
tunes of the town, in the later third and fourth centuries. At the northern
end of the town excavations in the 1970s revealed a picture of quite intense
activity; this seems to have been firmly based on industry and manufactur-
ing in the fourth century. There was an agglomeration of superimposed
remains of many buildings and occupation layers possibly spanning some
100 years or more (Plate 24). The structures ranged from simple stake-
supported wattle and daub sheds and outhouses, to more substantial rec-

PLATE 23. During the excavations regular guided tours were organized for the staff. Here
          a party is being shown the pottery kiln and associated features.

tangular timber-framed buildings. In the earlier phases most of these buildings were fronting onto Ermine Street, though there was plenty of evidence
for structures in the areas behind the larger streetside buildings. An interesting aspect of this later occupation was the large amount of progressive
encroachment onto the margins and even the central agger of Ermine Street.

PLATE 24. Looking west from Ermine Street a palimpsest of features are visible. Most of
          these relate to the later industrial phases. Note the patched and repaired surface
          of Ermine Street at the bottom of the photograph.

At its original full width the Street was some 8 metres wide, between the shallow drainage ditches. During the closing years of the occupation the ditches were filled in and encroachment from both sides had narrowed the gap to only some 4 or 5 metres of usable surface. One building in particular was of considerable interest. Constructed probably in the late third century it was built partly over the western drainage ditch of Ermine Street. In plan it was perfectly square – 4 x 4 metres – with four massive stone-filled post-pits at the corners. Midway between the main corner posts were four smaller intermediate post-holes (see Plate 25). A number of items found associated with this structure are considered to be of religious significance. For example, three triple vases, thought to be used as incense burners and altar lamps, some fragments of thin bronze plates, often found as votive offerings in Roman temples, and a considerable scatter of small denomination bronze coins. All these were recovered from the layer of silt that had accumulated between the front of the building and Ermine Street. Also, from the fill of the north-western stone packed post-hole, came most of the remains of a horse skull (Plate 26). Just to the rear of this square building a small arc of baby burials were found (perhaps some of the female baby 'exposures'). These finds recall many other finds of like material from Roman Britain, which are associated with Romano-Celtic temples. Horse and/or ox skulls were often buried as foundation offerings when these

PLATE 25.   A small Roman temple on the west side of Ermine Street, looking north. The large hole at the bottom of the photograph is a modern soakaway. The layers of chalk and gravel, seen partway down in the hole, represent earlier phases of buildings

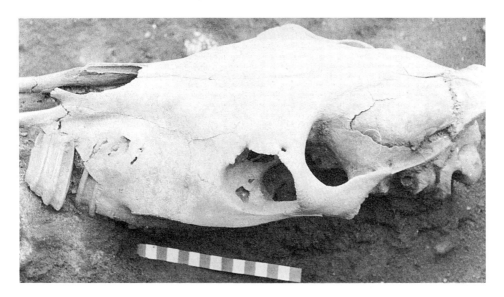

PLATE 26. A large horse skull recovered from the fill of the north-west stone packed post-
hole of the temple. Note the large teeth at the left hand side of the jaw.

square, cella-style temples were built. The likeness to the building found
beside the Ermine Street on the south side of the river will no doubt impress
itself on the reader. It is difficult to estimate exactly how long this temple
(or roadside shrine) survived in use but it was eventually swept away
and superseded by at least three more phases of buildings, all of them
progressively creeping eastwards onto and over the edges of Ermine Street.

    To the west and behind the main ranges of street front buildings, large
areas of cobbled yards were found. Many rather scruffy, lightly built structures were scattered around these areas (Plate 27). A square timber-lined
well was associated with some phases of these cobbled yards; but by the
latest phase the well had been backfilled and was covered by another layer
of cobbling. The contents of the well may have had something to do with
the filling in and covering of it. At the bottom of the well the waterlogged
remains of the timber lining was still in place (see Plate 28). Lying at the
bottom of the shaft were numerous articulated skeletons of pigs and dogs
(Plate 29). These must have either fallen in (most unlikely considering the
number) or been deliberately thrown in. Does this mean that there had
been some outbreak of something like 'foot and mouth', or 'swinefever'?
Otherwise it is difficult to account for such useful food carcasses (the pigs
anyway) being discarded in such a wasteful manner. Perhaps it was the
obnoxious smell, from the decaying carcasses, that precipitated the infilling
of the well.

PLATE 27. This is a composite photogram of the multitude of features present in the latest phases of the Roman town. Recorded in 5m squares the total excavated area is some 35 x 15 metres. On the right hand side is Ermine Street with some of the large post-holes and the street frontages of buildings on the east side.

PLATE 28. Despite being filled and buried for over 1,500 years the timber lining of the
Roman well was still intact at the base of the shaft.

There may, of course, have been a more sinister reason for the contents
of the well – what if a marauding band of Saxons had descended on
the unprotected town? Pillaging, raping and killing anyone or anything
unfortunate enough not to have taken refuge in the forests or marshes of
the surrounding countryside. This incident may have been the beginning
of the end for the Romano-British town. We know that there must have
been survivors because the, probably rotting, corpses had been collected
and dumped in the well. This also may account for the rather scruffy
inhumations discovered in 1987 (see p. 38) close to the river to the south-
west of the town. After the filling of the well another cobble layer had been
laid down and there was also evidence for two or three further phases of
occupation; despite the apparent activity none of this very late occupation
is in any way substantial. The structures were scrappy affairs with light
post-holes and wattle and daub walls, with rudimentary floors of gravel or
beaten earth. The whole aspect of the occupation seems to change from the
time the well was backfilled.

PLATE 29. The skeleton of a pig can be seen lying in the bottom of the well. The large flints visible may have been thrown in to sink the carcass.

PLATE 30. Small oval-shaped iron smelting furnace. It has been cut into the side of a small rectangular furnace.

We leave the readers to draw their own conclusions about the goings on in the twilight years of the Roman town – plague and pestilence or marauding Saxons. Personally we are inclined towards the Saxon raiders, somehow it seems a more exciting and appropriate ending.

During the latter part of the town's life much of this northern sector seems to have been given over to industry. Many small ore roasting ovens and smelting furnaces were discovered (see Plate 30). In one place a scatter of bronze coin blanks (unstruck discs) were found. Perhaps one of the illegal practices of these early 'Wareites' was coin forging! More legitimate activity is attested by the discovery of unfinished or part-finished objects of bronze. In other areas quantities of bone waste and part-finished bone objects pinpoint the workshops of bone craftsmen. There was, apparently, also a thriving business in the preparation of grain for breadmaking. Many broken and part-worn fragments of querns and millstones (some made from Andernach lava imported from Germany) were found. Important as they were in their own way, these smaller craftsmen-based activities were overshadowed by what appears to have been a very thriving ironworking industry. Masses of waste from ore reduction and smelting was widely scattered across the large open areas of cobbled yards. The ovens and smelting furnaces being mainly set into the cobbles. Larger, rectangular, smithing shafts may have been used as forges to work the iron into the finished products. Several of these large furnaces had raised areas of heavy cobbles close to them – these may have supported water tanks for 'plunging' the iron, or perhaps were the bases for anvils to stand on (Plate 31). The late Professor Ron Tylecote, an expert on early metallurgy, examined a selection of the knives, chisels, saws and

PLATE 31. Several smithing furnaces and roasting ovens can be seen in this picture. A flint support, probably for a 'plunging' tank, is at the bottom.

choppers that were found. He pronounced the products to be of excellent quality: on testing most of the tools were found to have a cutting edge of good quality, low grade steel. Also of considerable interest were the large number of damaged and part-worn iron 'hipposandals' found beside the Ermine Street. These sandals, or ox-shoes (see Fig. 10, p. 62) are discussed and described in more detail later in the chapter where the possible connection between the ironworkers of Ware town and Foxholes Farm is explored further.

What is especially impressive is the evidence for a wide range of imports, still arriving from the Continent in the fourth century (Fig. 8). In addition to the imported lava querns and millstones, we have many examples of Mayan Wares – a distinctive type of pottery from Germany – and Rhenish glasswares. Some of the late metalwork and other artefacts are also likely

FIGURE 8.   Map of Britain and Europe showing the routes by which material was coming to Ware in the fourth century.

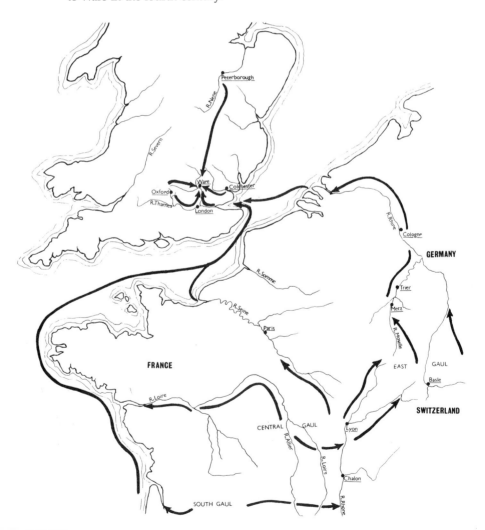

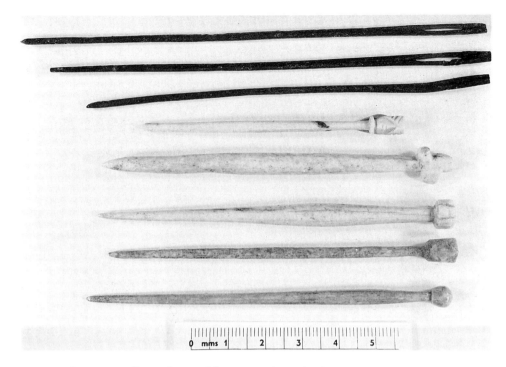

PLATE 32. Bronze needles and carved bone pins from the Roman town.

to have been imported. What was it that made Ware important enough still to be attracting traders, or at least trade goods, from abroad (Plates 32, 33, 34 & 35) at a time when many Roman towns were in total decline?

PLATE 33. A bronze 'oyster' spoon, bronze steelyard and a decorated bone handle with an iron tang still inside, from the Roman town.

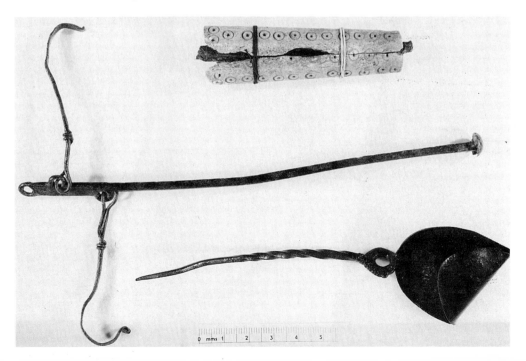

PLATE 34. Two very fine enamelled bronze brooches from the Roman town. One is of cruciform type, with red and yellow enamel vandyke decoration. The other is in the form of a bee with enamel panels on the wings.

PLATE 35. Bronze objects from the Roman town. A finger ring with a padlock key attached and a ladies' toilet set with ear scoop, nail cleaner and a pair of tweezers.

HERTFORD IN ROMAN TIMES?

Can we really talk about 'Roman' Hertford? Hertford is certainly not on the alignment of any major Roman road, though it has been suggested (Viatores: *Roman Roads in the South-East Midlands*, 1964) that there was a valley road south of the Lea, coming in via Hertingfordbury and running approximately along the line of present day West Street before proceeding from Hertford to Ware on the line of the present Ware Road.

Apart from this, largely unproven, road and some late Roman burials found in the Mangrove Road area the evidence for Roman Hertford is very slim. There have been a few scattered finds of Roman pottery in the vicinity of the Castle and Green Dragon Yard but nothing of any consequence to suggest occupation, on anything more than a very limited scale. In 1990 excavations by the Hertfordshire Archaeological Trust at Old Cross, close to the river, did reveal Roman material of enough substance to suggest that there may indeed have been a small riverside settlement close by the ford at Hertford.

The evidence at Old Cross consisted of a dark occupation layer just above the natural subsoil. This layer, some half metre thick, produced thirty odd sherds of Roman samian pottery. Associated with this layer was a row of fairly substantial post- holes. These post-holes were laid out at a right angle to the line of the river and it is possible that they may have originally formed part of a bridge, or been a hand rail, to assist pedestrians in crossing the ford at this point (Plate 36). The limits of the excavation precluded a more extensive investigation and the origins and purpose of any structure these post-holes were associated with, must remain a matter for conjecture.

A pit for a cremation burial (described earlier, see Plate 9, p. 27) was cut into the original ground surface and appeared to be, at least partly, sealed by the ?Roman occupation layer. Though described as Late Iron Age the burial probably dates from the years following the Roman Conquest. We could possibly be looking at evidence for some Late Iron Age activity, starting just before and continuing on into the Roman period.

The finds generally from this site range from the mid-first through to the fourth century AD. A smaller excavation at the rear of 54 St Andrew Street also produced some evidence of occupation in the first and second centuries AD.

We are grateful to Hester Cooper-Reade, the Site Director for the Trust on both of these sites, for her comments. Her personal feeling is that the evidence recovered from these two sites does confirm some Roman and

PLATE 36. Bases of wooden posts found at Millbridge, Hertford.

possibly Late Iron Age occupation in the St Andrew Street area; and possibly even on both sides of the ford.

Obviously the occupation was not of a very intensive nature and probably never amounted to anything much more than a few households clustered around the ford. Nevertheless, the quality of the pottery recovered points to it being a bit better than a rural slum. So maybe we are looking at something like a small custodial establishment guarding the ford or, possibly, there may have been a Roman corn mill thereabouts. Certainly by Domesday, albeit some eight to nine centuries later, Hertford had three mills in operation. The confluence of several rivers at Hertford would provide ideal conditions for water mills.

FOXHOLES FARM SITE

In addition to the nucleated Roman town at Ware, excavations at Foxholes Farm, south of Ware, uncovered the remains of an extensive open settlement, dating from the third century AD. The economy of this upland settlement seems to have been firmly based on agriculture, with a flourishing sideline in metal working. The remaining traces of fields, enclosures and drove roads are an indication of fairly intensive stock rearing and agriculture. Several corndrying/malting ovens were found and are probably indicative of the uncertain weather conditions in late Roman Britain (Plates 37 & 38). Corn which had to be harvested in damp conditions would have been dried in the ovens to stop it going mouldy during the winter storage (Fig. 9). It is interesting at this point in the story to expand a little on the malting function that some, if not all, the corndryers at Foxholes Farm fulfilled. A replica of the best preserved of the Foxholes corndryers was reconstructed at the Butser Ancient Farm Project Centre, in Hampshire (Plate 39, see also Col Plate IV). Experiments with hulled barley had surprising results. Rather than simply drying the corn, as had been expected, the experiments eventually

PLATE 37. A well preserved corndrying oven, found at Foxholes Farm.

Colour Plate IV. An artistic representation of the Roman corndryers in action at Foxholes Farm. Painted by Tony Meadows.

PLATE 38. Details of the internal flue arrangements. This oven was subsequently removed
from the site and conserved and is on display (by appointment with Hertford
Museum) in the old Seed Warehouse at Old Cross, Hertford.

succeeded in producing a good quantity of high class brewing malt. In fact
a local Hampshire brewery made a few barrels of very drinkable ale using
the Butser malt. Were the Foxholes Farm maltsters the forerunners of the
celebrated malting families that made Ware and Hertford so famous in later
years? Ware was a malting town from early years. The Benedictine monks
of the Alien Priory made their own malt for brewing. In fact it is said that
the old Canon Maltings stood on the site of the original Benedictine malt-
house. Daniel Defoe in 1724 mentions Ware as one of the towns from whence
came the vast quantities of malt – known as Hertfordshire Malt – that was
regarded as 'the best in all England'. During the heyday of the malting
industry both Ware and Hertford must have been dominated by a skyline
of the distinctive oasthouse cowls.

At some stage, probably during the fourth century, a community of metal
workers seems to have set up shop alongside the farmers, maltsters and
stock rearers. We now find the remains of smelting furnaces and ore roasting

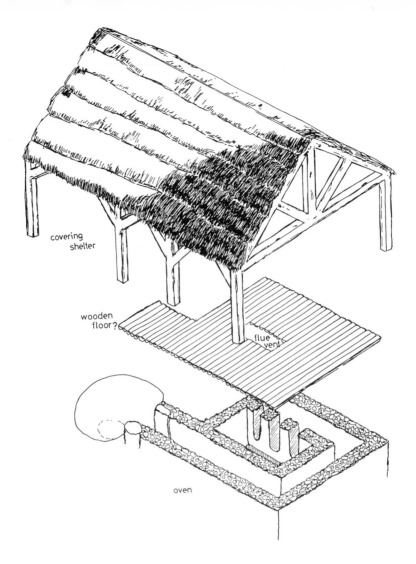

FIGURE 9.   An exploded sketch of the suggested elements from the Foxholes Farm corndryer/malting oven.

ovens side by side with the corndryers. Were these people really newcomers? Or is it more likely that the former farming community is starting to diversify in response to the growing demand for iron products? In the town at Ware a similar upsurge in ironworking is very apparent at this time. In addition to many other iron objects dozens of fragments from worn and broken 'hipposandals' were discovered on the west side of Ermine Street, at the north end of the town. Could it be that the more settled economic conditions in the early fourth century led to an increase in long distance trade? Certainly during the fourth century Continental imports of pottery

PLATE 39. A full-scale working model of the Foxholes Farm corndryer was reconstructed at Butser Ancient Farm, Hampshire.

and possibly olive oil and even wine, were still reaching Ware. The many fragments of 'hipposandals' found beside the Roman road suggests that there was a brisk trade in those strange bootlike objects, that were used to protect the hooves of the draught oxen. The flattened plate part was slipped under the hoof and the two side tangs were tapped in to fit the hoof snugly. Finally leather thongs were secured to the loop at the front of the shoe and tied round the lower part of the oxens' legs (see Fig. 10). Oxen and not horses were the usual draught animals employed in hauling the heavy carts along the roads. The very nature of Roman roads, with the top surface composed of cobbles or coarse gravel, would have been extremely abrasive. Even with the iron 'protectors' on their feet it is difficult to imagine that oxen could go many miles without having to be reshod. Maybe the life of a 'hipposandal', with the inherent heavy wear and tear, was approximately twenty miles. Perhaps Ware may have been not only the first stop on the road north from London for the Imperial Post, but the first reshoeing stop for the oxcart teams!

We can deduce from the foregoing that what may seem at first glance to be two very diverse ways of life for the 'townies' of Ware and the 'bumpkins' of Foxholes Farm, do indeed have very much in common and probably all

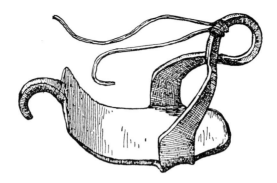

F<small>IGURE</small> 10.　Sketch of an iron 'hipposandal'; the leather thongs were probably long enough to wrap round the ox's lower leg, secured by the hook at the back.

were motivated by the needs of the market-place. It may be that the iron-workers of Ware town were the ones producing the finished ironwork necessary to service the oxcart caravans. But they, in turn, may have relied on the smelters and founders of Foxholes Farm to provide them with the raw materials.

4

The Post-Roman Period and the Coming of the Saxons

The area in Hertfordshire and adjoining Buckinghamshire that runs from the foot of the Chilterns to the Thames has produced very little evidence, apart from a few chance finds, for early Saxon occupation before about AD 600. A hut or house found at Stevenage was said to be of this date, a cremation burial, found at Furneaux Pelham, was furnished with pots, iron knives and spear heads of fifth–sixth century date. The whole of this area seems to be devoid of pagan Saxon cemeteries or centres of settlement, such as those in neighbouring Essex, Norfolk, Cambridgeshire and Bedfordshire.

Unfortunately archaeology is almost as reticent about Romano-British survival beyond *c.* AD 400. At Verulamium there appears to have been at least some reasonable amount of post-Roman occupation. At Ware three phases of occupation postdate the latest Roman layers from about AD 400. It is possible that at both sites occupation continued up to at least AD 500. No burials dating certainly to this period have been recognized to date, but as the population was mainly Christian by this time and grave goods are not normally found, how would one know them?

We do, however, have a certain amount of other evidence for this postulated survival. Firstly, Bede's *Ecclesiastical History of the English Nation* relates how St Germanus, Bishop of Troyes in Gaul, sailed to Britain in AD 429 and visited St Albans to refute a British heresy. He returned by invitation in AD 447 and had a peaceful and prosperous visit. Secondly, the evidence of place names. There is a strong survival of Celtic and Romano-British or Brythonic names in our area: Chiltern, Lea, Mimram, Colne, Beane and many others. The name Beane is very important. It derives from *'bene ficcan'*, the little goddess, with the adjective *'ficcan'* placed after the noun. This word order did not happen in Brythonic or Old Welsh until around AD 650 so perhaps we still have Celtic-speaking people naming the Beane around that time, over 200 years after the Romans had left. There are a number of names like Walden which are English but mean where the Welsh lived. Generally speaking, in our area there is a singular lack of early Saxon place names, whereas in East Anglia they are fairly common.

Together this evidence seems to point to an area between the Thames and the Chilterns staying relatively free from early Saxon penetration and settlement. In AD 571 the West Saxons and the Saxons from Cambridge defeated the Britons at the battle of Bedford and captured Aylesbury. If the Britons they were fighting were the lower Chiltern and Thames Valley Britons, it may indicate that the descendants of Romano-British peoples could have continued to live in our area down to at least the end of the sixth century, relatively untroubled by the Saxon invaders. It was only in the seventh century that this Chiltern enclave became Anglicized.

Of course we have no way of knowing how strong this supposed British enclave was. Exactly what numbers were involved is not clear. The Britons may have been gradually reduced, due to unfavourable economic conditions, or possibly some plague or pestilence. But the likelihood is that our generally fertile area, which supported a large population in the Iron Age and Roman period, continued to be reasonably well populated in the fifth and sixth centuries by surviving Romano-Britons. These people were likely to have been Christian, for certainly our area would look to Verulamium as the centre of Christianity in the late Roman period.

HERTFORD

The two earliest written references we have to Hertford are the Venerable Bede's account of the Synod held at Hertford in AD 673 and the entries in the Anglo-Saxon Chronicle, recording the construction, by King Edward the Elder, of twin *burghs* at Hertford in AD 912/13.

Identification of our Hertford with the Synod 'Herutford' is in some dispute (see discussion of this point by Sal Garfi in Appendix A). However, if it was our Hertford, it must at least presuppose some reasonable amount of settlement here before AD 673. It is most unlikely that the bishops would meet at a deserted site near a ford, for if they had why would Bede say 'We met at a place called Herutford . . .', indicating that the name had significance.

Part of the entry from Bede's *Ecclesiastical History* is worth quoting here: 'We met on the 24th day of September at a place called Herutford (myself [Theodore] the unworthy Bishop of the See of Canterbury appointed by the Apostolic See), our fellow priest Bisi, Bishop of the East Angles also by his proxies, Wilfrid, Bishop of the Nation of Northumbrians, Putta, Bishop of Rochester, Eleutherius, Bishop of the West Saxons and Winfred, Bishop of the Province of the Mercians . . .' This historic meeting, whether at our Hertford or some other, was the real cornerstone of the establishment of the

English Church. It set out the episcopal nature of that Church as opposed to the looser Celtic Church or the monastic Christianity of Ireland.

In any case there is no doubt that the *burghs* of AD 912/13 belong to our Hertford. The Anglo-Saxon Chronicle refers to the Northern *burgh* as lying between 'the Maran and the Beane and the Lea'. It seems likely that there was some pre-*burgh* settlement – unless, of course, the *burghs* really were just military establishments with no pretention to civil status, at least in the early period. It is therefore important for our discussions to establish whether occupation continued from the Roman period onwards or if not, when the Saxon settlement started.

While the Roman causeway and bridge remained in use at Ware the importance of the ford at Hertford was minimal. However, once the crossing at Ware became unusable traffic between London and the north, using the Roman Ermine Street, would probably have diverted to the ford at Hertford. From there the natural route would have been up Port Hill to head north-east to rejoin Ermine Street somewhere north of Ware. We have no direct evidence for the date when the crossing at Ware became impassable. We can, however, draw some conclusions from the negative evidence. First of all, the very name Ware probably comes from the English or Saxon name for weir (*wair* or *wodrash*) meaning an obstruction in the river – could this have been the remains of the Roman bridge and causeway? If so the bridge would have collapsed and obstructed the river by the time the Saxons arrived, possibly before AD 600.

At Millbridge, Hertford, the Roman occupation levels were found to be overlaid by a thick layer of alluvium. Similarly, during emergency excavations in 1976 at Ware Lock, the Roman levels were also found to be covered by a thick layer of alluvium and peat. This suggests that sometime fairly soon after the end of the Roman period substantial flooding took place, possibly for a considerable period of time. This may have been due to a general rise in the water level perhaps indicating a deterioration in the climatic conditions. This could have contributed to the downfall of the Roman bridge. It is our personal feeling that the Roman bridge finally ceased to be of use somewhere between AD 500 and 600 and thereafter the ford at Hertford gradually developed as the main crossing point, at least for a couple of hundred years or so.

As we have already said, the surviving Romano-British population in our area is likely to have embraced Christianity. Christian preaching crosses are a feature of the early Celtic Church. There are well known examples still in existence today, though these are mainly confined to sparsely populated areas in the west and the north of the British Isles. Hertford originally had two crosses, one at Old Cross on the north side of the river and one in the old Market Place close to the present Shire Hall. The position of both are recorded on the earliest maps of Hertford, Speed's (1610) and Norden's (1621). These preaching crosses would, in effect, have acted as the first churches, except that the congregation would not have had the luxury of a roof over their heads. Some of these crosses might date back perhaps to the sixth century, before the arrival of St Augustine's mission to found the English Church at Canterbury in AD 597. In our area they may have been the out-preaching stations of the known Christian Church at St Albans.

During sewer work in the area of the old Market Place, on the west side of the Shire Hall in 1975, a considerable number of burials were unearthed. These were recorded and rescued by Elisabeth Barratt, then the Assistant Curator at Hertford Museum and were subsequently judged to be of late Saxon date (E.Barratt: *Hertfordshire Archaeological Review* 10, 1976). Again, in 1988, during renovation work on the Shire Hall itself, a quantity of human bones were unearthed by the Hertfordshire Archaeological Trust; these particular bones, consisting of several individuals, were largely disarticulated and it would appear that the original burials had been moved and reburied. This could have occurred when the Southern *burgh* was founded in AD 913, or, more likely, when the foundations for the Shire Hall were laid out in 1769. All these interments were almost certainly related to a fairly extensive cemetery which must have been around the outer periphery of the old Market Place – a not uncommon arrangement in late Saxon and early Medieval times.

Excavations north of the river, in the area of the Northern *burgh*, have been limited to three investigations carried out by the Hertfordshire Archaeological Trust; at Millbridge near the river; behind 4/6 St Andrew Street and at the back of 54 St Andrew Street. As we have already noted, at Millbridge the Roman levels were overlaid by thick layers of silt and mud. Above this sterile layer the archaeological evidence suggests occupation no earlier than the tenth or eleventh century. At the other two sites, slightly further north along St Andrew Street, the picture was broadly the same.

In the Southern *burgh* archaeological work has been more extensive. There have been excavations in Castle Street, Green Dragon Yard, Maidenhead Street, Honey Lane and in the Railway Street/Bircherley Green area in particular. But it has to be said that none of these has produced evidence for occupation which could be said to be definitely earlier than the tenth century.

The only site anywhere in close proximity to Hertford to produce evidence for Saxon occupation that is earlier than this is at Foxholes Farm, just to the south-east of Hertford, towards Hertford Heath. Here during extensive excavations Saxon buildings were found. There were some six or seven sunken-floored huts, rectangular in plan (see Plates 40, 41 & 42) with evidence of internal hearths and the typical opposed large post-holes which

PLATE 40. A Saxon sunken-floored building under excavation at Foxholes Farm, Hertford.

supported the roofs (Plate 43). A quantity of grass-tempered pottery was found in the fill of these huts, along with a small Saxon-type knife. In addition to these smaller huts several much larger structures of hall-like

PLATE 41. A rectangular Saxon hut at Foxholes Farm, with substantial post-holes at either end.

PLATE 42. A large rectangular building at Foxholes Farm, with large opposing post-holes and smaller ones along the sides.

PLATE 43. Reconstructed sunken-floored buildings at West Stow Saxon village, in Suffolk.

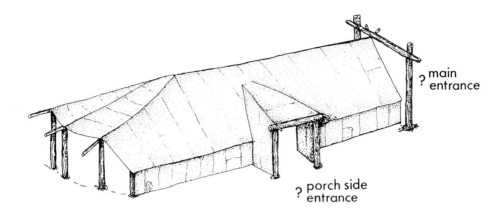

? main
entrance

? porch side
entrance

FIGURE 11. A suggested reconstruction of one of the large Saxon hall-like buildings at Foxholes Farm. They could have been rather like the marquees used today on showgrounds.

size were found. From the lack of any quantity of occupation debris it would seem that these buildings were in use for a fairly short time.

Clive Partridge, who directed the excavations, suggests that there is a possibility this site could have been connected with the Synod of AD 673; if, in fact, our Hertford really did host the Synod. The halls and huts may have housed the various bishops and their entourages. The short-lived nature of the occupation and the date range of the artefacts would certainly fit with such an interpretation. The huts and the halls would have been just about sufficient to house the attending Bishops' households (Fig. 11). The site at Foxholes is on a dry, well-drained, gravel spur and it lies just off the line of the Roman road on the way to the ford.

If we do accept that our Hertford was the place of this Synod the settlement that must have existed here may well have owed its foundation to the demise of the old Roman bridge at Ware.

WARE

Evidence for Romano-British survival into the post-Roman period is non-existent at Hertford, but at Ware the situation is somewhat different. The extensive excavations on the Glaxo site have yielded very important evidence for continuity of occupations at least into the fifth century. On top of the latest 'Roman' layers there were several more phases of wooden structures. Individually these phases were not closely datable in themselves, as only residual late Roman material was associated with them. But if we allow something in the region of twenty to thirty years for each phase it is easy to see that occupation could have continued well into the fifth century AD at least. These later structures were the last in a series of encroachments over the surface of the Ermine Street starting probably in the early fourth century. Eventually the usable width of the road was narrowed to only some 4 metres. These later timber buildings may have overhung the street much like Medieval buildings with the first storey jutting out above a pedestrian walkway below. This was a far cry from the original Roman plan with the road some 8 to 10 metres wide. A similar situation was discovered at the Roman town of Uriconium, near Shrewsbury in Shropshire. Excavations there revealed a whole series of structures postdating the latest datable Roman phases. And these, like those at Ware, had been built out over streets with what look like old-fashioned Wild West boardwalks along the edges of the streets. At Ware there was also a series of large post-holes crossing the centre of the road in what appears to have been the latest phase. This may be evidence for some sort of barrier erected to stop, or regulate, traffic trying to enter the town from the north (Plate 44).

PLATE 44.   This photograph shows buildings encroaching onto the east side of Ermine Street, at Glaxo's. Some of the large stone packed post-holes can be seen with ranging rods inserted into them.

PLATE 45. Large post-holes and shallow pits of post-Roman date at Ware Library.

We have already mentioned the possible small temple and/or toll house found on the south bank of the Lea, where occupation may also have extended into the post-Roman period. There also the later structures had spread over the original road ditches and encroached on the road. In 1978 excavations on the site of a proposed extension to Ware Library revealed some late, or post-Roman structures, along with late Roman pottery and a few sherds of grass-tempered wares of possible mid-Saxon date. The evidence for at least some modicum of Saxon activity in the late sixth or seventh centuries is sparse and fairly widely scattered, but it is there (Plate 45). To the north of the Library site, on both sides of present day Baldock Street, excavations by the Hart Archaeological Unit recovered fairly substantial quantities of late Saxon pottery and evidence for contemporary buildings.

In general, the evidence suggests that the Romano-Britons continued living in the Roman town at least throughout the fifth century. Then at some unknown time, perhaps in the later sixth century, Saxon peoples arrived, choosing to settle in the area to the east of the Roman town, as Saxons were known to be reluctant to occupy previously built-up areas. They may even have lived peacefully side by side with the surviving Britons for a while.

Eventually the population of the old Roman town dwindled and the remnants may have moved out, leaving the future history of Ware in the hands of Saxon newcomers. After all, if, as we have suggested, the Roman bridge had become unusable there would have been little point in continuing to live in a decaying town on the north side of a non-existent bridge. The collapsed remains of that bridge, which might well have been substantial with large pile-like supports in the river bed, may have formed an obstruction to the passage of boats using the river above Ware. Any such obstruction would have made navigation virtually impossible beyond Ware and this would have enhanced Ware's position as a river port.

The date of the bridge's demise may well lie in the sixth century. This would fit well with what we suspect about the period of surviving occupation at the old Roman town. This also equates well with the arrival in Ware of Saxon pottery, coins and metalwork in perhaps the sixth or early seventh century.

These events are significant not only for Ware, but also for Hertford. Once the bridge had gone the Roman road through Ware was no longer a viable route and traffic would probably have left the Ermine Street, somewhere near to where the War Memorial stands at Hertford Heath, and diverted to ford the river at Hertford. This, for the first time, would have seen the rise of Hertford at Ware's expense.

From the excavations at the Ware Library site came Saxon grass-tempered pottery of possible sixth to eighth-century date, some post-holes and possible floors of similar date. Exploratory excavations at the Secret Garden site – between Ware High Street and the Gazebos along the river frontage – were carried out by the Hertfordshire Archaeological Trust in 1987 mainly to evaluate the potential of the area before the proposed development. Remnants of Saxon riverside structures were found and, among other artefacts, a fine bronze strap end, decorated and inlaid with patterns in silver (see Frontispiece). It is of a type popular in the sixth to eighth centuries AD. Further investigations of this area awaits a discussion on the development. Should the development go ahead the opportunity to conduct a detailed examination of this, potentially most important area, must not be missed. At No. 3 West Street a Saxon penny, or *sceatta* of sixth-century type was found (Plate 46).

In addition to these sites Saxon grass-tempered and plainware pottery was recovered from the excavations on both sides of Baldock Street. However, there, the main thrust of occupation seems to have been of ninth to tenth-century date. On both these Baldock Street sites there was evidence of pre-Medieval structures (Plate 47). When all this evidence is looked at closely it seems to suggest that, in the sixth–seventh centuries, there was some Saxon occupation in the area between the present High Street and the

PLATE 46. Top in the photograph is a Saxon silver penny (*sceatta*) from 3 West Street, Ware. It is slightly smaller than a modern 5p piece. The two coins underneath are of Late Iron Age date from the excavations at Glaxo's. Ware Museum.

PLATE 47. Excavations at 13–23 Baldock Street, Ware. At the bottom are the remains of an early Medieval building. To the top and right the walls of a later Medieval building can be seen. The post-holes and slots of late Saxon structures were revealed when the floors of the later buildings were removed.

PLATE 48.   Excavations to the rear of Waggoners Yard, Ware, revealed the remains of World
War II air raid shelters. Also, running across the centre of the site, was a Victorian
brick culvert containing the ancient stream of the Upper Bourne.

river. Later on this seems to have become more formalized into a village-
like settlement centred on the Baldock Street area. This area forms a perfect
natural settlement site. We have a low, gradually rising, gravel plateau
bounded to the east and west by two small streams, called Lower Bourne
and Upper Bourne (see Plate 48), which originally ran down from the low
chalk hills to the north and joined the Lea on either side of the present
priory grounds. With the river to the south any settlement here would have
been well set up and congenial, with easy access to the river and the
hinterland.

Before moving on it is interesting to review the events of the late ninth
century. The Anglo-Saxon Chronicle tells us that in AD 871 Alfred became
King of Wessex and for twenty years fought against the Danish invaders.
By AD 890 he had succeeded in halting the Danish invasion of Wessex and
had gone over to the offensive, capturing London. However, fighting still
continued and in AD 895 the Anglo-Saxon Chronicle states that

> The aforementioned host [of Danes] built a fort by the river Lea twenty miles
> above the City of London. Then later in the summer a large body of the
> garrison [of London] and of other [Saxon] forces set out and reached the Danish
> fort and there they were repulsed and some four of the King's Thanes were
> slain.

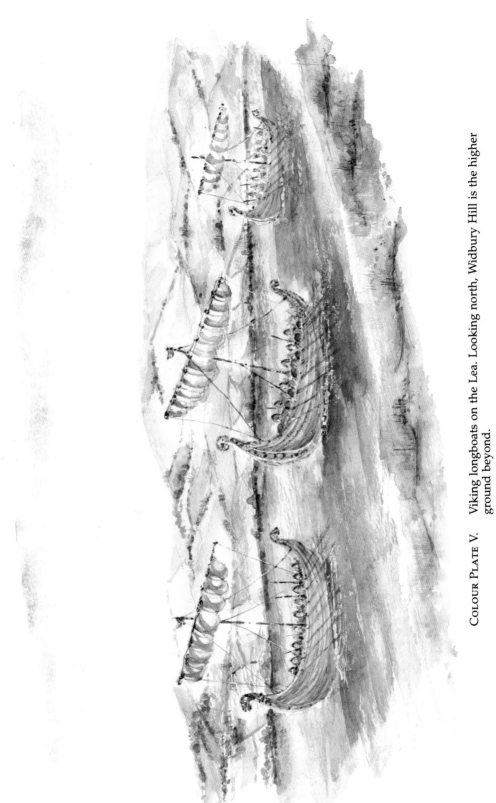

COLOUR PLATE V.   Viking longboats on the Lea. Looking north, Widbury Hill is the higher ground beyond.

... Then the following autumn [presumably of the same year] the King encamped in the neighbourhood of the fortress while the corn was being reaped so that the Danish men could not keep them back from the reaping. One day the King rode up along the river and looked to see where it could be blocked so that [the Danes] would not be able to bring out their ships. This [the Saxons] proceeded to do; they made two forts on the two sides of the river, but when they had just begun that operation and had encamped thereby, the host saw that they could not bring out their ships. Thereupon they abandoned them and went across country until they reached Bridgnorth in Severn.

This was one of Alfred's greatest victories; it was the culmination of twenty-five years of fighting, because after this victory the Danish host began to evaporate and never really threatened Wessex again. An entry in the Anglo-Saxon Chronicle for AD 896 states '... in this year the host dispersed some to East Anglia, some to Northumbria, and those without stock got themselves ships and sailed south oversea to the Seine. The host, by the mercy of God, had not altogether utterly crushed the English people: but they [the Danes] were much more severely crushed.'

It has been suggested that the entries above refer to events at Hertford (Plate 49). But a more likely interpretation is that the Danes sailed up the Lea to Ware (Plate 50 & Fig. 12). There they found the river obstructed by the 'Weir' (see Col. Plate V). So they set up camp somewhere close at hand, where they would have good communication routes to the rich farmlands north of the Lea for their provisions. Alfred trapped them there and forced them to flee overland. Of his two forts, which if begun were never completed, there remains no sign. Where were they sited? It has been suggested that one of the forts may have been at Hertford with the other perhaps at Stanstead Abbotts, trapping the Danes between them (for further discussion of this see Appendix D).

Did the people who lived in those houses that we found traces of in Baldock Street, witness these stirring events – did they, in fact, participate?

PLATE 49.   A Viking sword found at Hertford. Hertford Museum.

PLATE 50. A Viking antler bodkin/talisman, found during the southern Ermine Street excavations in 1974 (see also Fig. 12).

Were they some of the local population that the Anglo-Saxon Chronicle tells of King Alfred protecting from the Danes at harvest time? Perhaps they headed the victory parade through the streets of Ware after the Danes fled.

There's no way we will ever be able to prove this, of course, but it is exciting to think that our excavations in Ware have perhaps brought us within touching distance of the stirring events of 895.

FIGURE 12. Drawing of the decoration on the Viking bodkin found at Ware. The square-section shaft has a different design on each side. The pointed end is carved and decorated to represent the head of a fish, perhaps a pike or salmon.

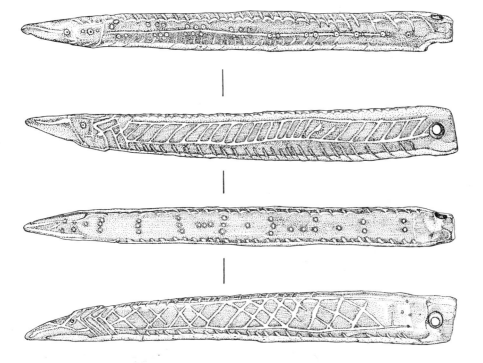

5

The Late Saxon Period

'In this year, after Martinmas, King Edward had the most northerly fortress at Hertford built between the Maran and the Beane and the Lea . . .' Edward moved with his army to Maldon and ' . . . Another part of his forces built the fortress at Hertford meanwhile on the southern bank of the Lea . . .' These are part of the entries in the Anglo-Saxon Chronicle for AD 912/13; proof of the foundations at Hertford. As we have discussed elsewhere, Hertford may possibly have existed as a settlement before that date but certainly from AD 912 it did positively exist, firstly as a military outpost, then as a civil town and later a borough. Before considering in detail the layout of the two *burghs* we should perhaps reflect on the historical reasons which led to them being built.

Alfred's defeat of the Danish host in AD 895 had saved southern and western England from Danish domination. In 901 Alfred died, leaving the kingdom to his son Edward. Edward the Elder, as he was to be called, was also a tough and shrewd fighter and Alfred's daughter Aethelflead was in the same mould. She was married to Aethelred the Saxon Ealdorman of Mercia (the old Saxon Kingdom of Mercia made famous under King Offa 200 years earlier had been overrun by the Danes. Alfred when he reconquered the area installed Aethelred as Earl, not King, and thus secured Wessex supremacy over Mercia). Aethelred's earldom, however, included London, Oxford and Hertford.

In AD 910 Edward, helped by Aethelred, had decisively beaten the Danes at the battle of Tettenhall and went over to the offensive against the remaining East Anglian and Northumbrian Danes. In AD 911 Aethelred died and thereafter Edward formally took over Mercian lands, though leaving his sister Aethelflead in charge. Brother and sister worked together as a brilliant team until her death in 918 and by the time of Edward's death in AD 924, virtually all of England had been reconquered. The conquests included north-east England, Strathclyde, south-east Scotland and all Northumbria up to Edinburgh. In 923 Edward was accepted by the king of the Scots as 'father and Lord'. So also did Raegnald and all the Northumbrians together with the king of the Strathclyde Welsh and all his subjects, though it was left to his son Aethelstan to complete and consolidate these conquests.

One of the first steps on Edward's path to these conquests was the fortification of Hertford. This was important for three reasons. Firstly, to secure London from attack. Secondly, it was vital as the first reasonable crossing-place of the Lea up from the Thames. Thirdly, to act as a base for his advance into East Anglia.

Edward was never a laggard and even as the fortifications were raised at Hertford he was off to beseige the Danes at Maldon and to build a fortress at Witham. Two years later he took and refortified Bedford. The full account of Edward's and Aethelflead's twelve years of campaigning against the Danelaw is a remarkable story – Hertford to Scotland – a most important chapter in English History.

Our area is now a relatively peaceful part of England but in the ninth and tenth centuries it was a frontier outpost in the Saxon–Danish Wars. Alfred saved the Saxon Kingdoms by his victory over the Danes, somewhere up the Lea, in AD 895. His son Edward, using as a springboard his fortresses at Hertford, started his recovery of the northern part of England from the Danes in AD 913. Is it possible that we can still identify the actual sites of these fortresses at Hertford?

THE NORTHERN BURGH AT HERTFORD

We are told that the Northern *burgh* was laid out between the Mimram, the Beane and the Lea; the Anglo-Saxon Chronicle is quite specific on that point (Fig. 13). Today the Mimram joins the Lea well west of the town in the water meadows close to Hertford Football Club. However, it is reasonable to suggest that in AD 912 the Mimram ran along the north side of those water meadows to join the Lea further to the north-east. That course today is marked by the ditch or stream which runs just to the south of St Andrews Church and the car park in St Andrew Street. It empties into the Lea in the castle grounds. If this assumption is correct it would then mean that the site of the Northern *burgh* was the Old Cross – St Andrew Street – Cowbridge area. There are a number of topographic clues which allow us to be more specific about this.

Firstly, it is important to remember that the *burgh's* boundaries or defences would consist of a ditch, water filled if possible, with an internal bank which may well have been palisaded with a wooden fighting platform and a walkway behind the palisade. Any buildings or properties within the *burgh* would finish at this walkway. Therefore, by looking at footpaths and property boundaries, along with the general lie of the land, some reasonable comments can be made.

If one starts at the river Lea, east of the public library at Old Cross, there

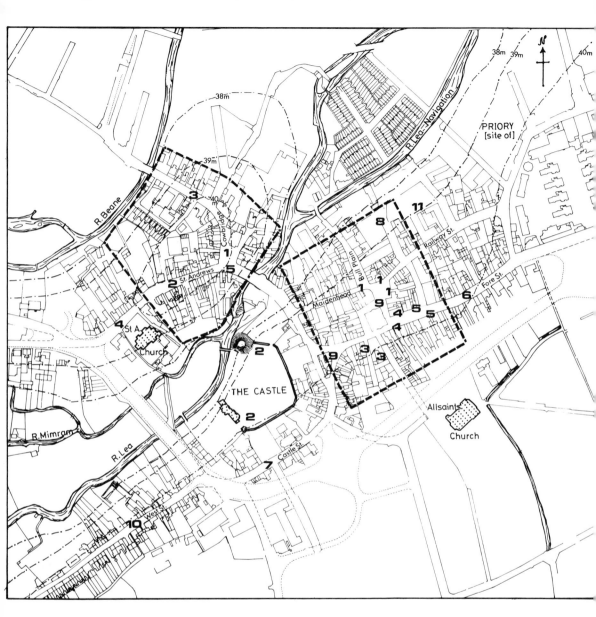

FIGURE 13.   Plan of Hertford based on the 1881 OS map. The suggested position of the
North and South *burghs* are indicated by the broad outlines. The contours
are shown to illustrate the way the ground rises on either side of the river.
The numbers represent Sal Garfi's Plan Units (See Appendix A).

is a narrow footpath running down to the river marking the boundary of Barber's yard. It is also noticeable that the ground in Barber's yard falls away very sharply to the north. Moving north-westward to Hartham Lane there is a high point with an abrupt falling away to the north or north-east. From that point north-westward to the Beane, just downstream from Cowbridge, the existing property boundaries facing Cowbridge all finish on a line. This alignment may give us the north-eastern boundary. Turning then south-westward to follow the Beane the remains of a large bank is still quite visible facing the Beane. We would then suggest at that point the boundary left the Beane and turned sharply to the south to cross St Andrew Street, just to the west of St Andrews churchyard where Cawthorne House now stands. The footpath, or twitchell, which runs from St Andrew Street, on the west side of St Andrews Church, could well mark the line of the original walkway behind the palisade. Where this twitchell crosses a stream (the old course of the Mimram?) the boundary sharply angles to the east to follow the Mimram's old course back to the Lea almost opposite Castle Hall. Alternatively the boundary linking the Beane and the Mimram may have been on the line of Brewhouse Lane to the south side of St Andrews Church (see Fig. 13).

In late Saxon times churches and their towers were sometimes incorporated as part of a *burgh's* defences and if there was, as we suspect, already a Saxon church at Old Cross (St Mary-the-Less), this may well have been so used. A former rector of St Andrews Church, the Rev. R. H. Gill, in his *Illustrated Guide to St Andrews Church* (1957), suggests that the foundation date of the original church on this spot was in the ninth century. We can find no evidence for such an early foundation date and think that it is more likely that St Andrews dates from the time of the early Medieval expansion – perhaps from the late twelfth century when the castle was being reconstructed and enlarged.

Relating these comments to Sal Garfi's units (see Appendix A), this suggested circuit for the *burgh* would include his Unit 1 – Old Cross itself, Unit 2 – St Andrew Street as far as St Andrews Church and Unit 3 – Cowbridge as far as the Beane. It also fits with his observation that St Andrew Street originally ended at Brewhouse Lane and that the west end of St Andrew Street and the area of Cowbridge, west of the Beane, would represent a Medieval expansion once the ditch and bank of the original *burgh* became redundant.

When we consider further the topography and chronology of this area it is valid to point out that Old Cross and the two roads, St Andrew Street and Cowbridge, have a rustic 'village' feel about them. That is, the pattern just developed naturally in the course of time and was not laid out in an orderly military fashion. It seems to us logical to suppose that either the pattern was already set when the *burgh* was laid out, then the outer ring of defences added to enclose it or, that the 'village' grew up within the abandoned fort. How much was originally enclosed by the defensive circuit is conjectural but one could suggest some, at least, of the buildings around Old Cross, with the Cross itself maybe still in position and possibly the early church of St Mary-the-Less. In addition, some of the development along the St Andrew Street and the Cowbridge frontages. Once the *burgh* was laid out (or the *burghal* circuit was still in place) these frontages would be fossilized and new developments along the two streets would naturally finish on the line of the old *burgh* boundaries.

How far back settlement began in the Old Cross area is uncertain but, bearing in mind the reservations expressed elsewhere in this narrative, it could in some form or another have been more or less continuous since Iron Age or Roman times. However, having said all that, we still have no definite evidence for Saxon occupation on the north side of the Lea before AD 912. Indeed, there is no archaeological evidence for anything as early as that date. So it is possible that the Northern *burgh* was not fully operational, in the sense of a fortress. It may be that it was abandoned soon after it was built, perhaps when the Southern *burgh* was finished.

THE SOUTHERN BURGH AT HERTFORD

The ditch forming the eastern boundary probably started from the Lea somewhere east of Lombard House, the present Hertford Club (Fig. 13). It then ran south across what was to become Bircherley Green, under Railway Street by the Duncombe Arms and Fore Street, just to the east side of the Dimsdale Arms. Taking the line of Post Office Passage it ran to All Saints churchyard. At this point, where the Ashbourne Ditch flowed into the *burgh* ditch, the boundary turned sharply to the west, possibly as far as Castle Street, where it then made another right angled turn to finish at the river Lea somewhere east of the present Castle grounds. This arrangement would have left a small tongue of land between the Lea and the Mimram outside the boundaries of either burgh. The evidence for the boundary ditch on the east side of the Southern *burgh* is clear. But it has to be said that from All Saints westward and then back to the Lea it is only guesswork (see Col. Plate VII, p. 111).

There is another piece of evidence which may have some bearing on our considerations. A little further to the west of the castle the remains of a bank and ditch can be seen in the water meadows, beyond the present Gascoyne Way. This can also be seen in section in the bank of the river Lea. The ditch and bank appears to run from West Street (about half way along) to the Beane, where it turns northward. Then it runs under the line of the present Gascoyne Way by Water's Garage. There is no evidence for the date of this ditch and bank. It could possibly be connected with the Saxon *burghs* or, more probably, some outwork associated with a later extension of defences when the castle was built, or even when Hertford was besieged – for example, in King John's reign when the French captured the castle. It is also possible that it relates to a time, in the early Middle Ages, when settlement expanded along West Street and also beyond the church in St Andrew Street.

The boundaries of the Southern *burgh*, as outlined above, conform quite well with Sal Garfi's Survey, equating with his Units 1, 2, 3, 4 and 8. In the Southern *burgh* the street layout is distinctly rectangular. It consists of two straight east–west streets – Maidenhead Street and the west end of Railway Street and Fore Street with side streets square to them, for example, Bull Plain, Green Street, Market Street, Bell Lane and Church Street. Of course the castle and its moat makes a curved incursion into this pattern at the west end but this was a Norman insertion. This regular pattern contrasts with the irregular 'village' street pattern of the Northern *burgh*. Whatever the status of the Northern *burgh*, the carefully laid out street plan of the Southern burgh leaves little doubt that something more formal and regular was intended here. The pattern of streets and gateways is reminiscent of a late Saxon planned town, such as Wallingford in Berkshire.

Was there really any settlement on the south side of the Lea before AD 912? We think that it is reasonable to suppose that there was, just as we have postulated some pre-*burgh* settlement on the north bank. If so where was it? We know from excavations at Honey Lane and Railway Street that the ground to the east was low-lying and may have been subjected to periodic flooding. Therefore, any settlement would have likely been clustered close to the ford and along the gravel ridge running down to the river from the Parliament Square direction.

It is likely that on its southern side the ford was quite shallow and wide and approached through 'The Wash' (so called because the shallows of the river would have been used for washing mud and dirt from carts and equipment – as well as the odd spot of laundry). There may have been houses and riverside structures and these may have extended as far as Maidenhead Street and possibly even as far as Parliament Square; encompassing the area of the Wash, Maidenhead Yard, Castle Hall and possibly part of Parliament Square.

In AD 913, when the *burgh* was laid out, the Maidenhead Street–Railway Street road alignment was laid out with gates possibly at both ends. Fore Street, as far as the Dimsdale Arms, may have been laid out at the same time, or possibly even as a secondary phase when the *burgh* assumed a

more civil role. This postulated southern 'pre-*burgh*' settlement may even
have had its own church. There are references to an early church dedicated
to St Nicholas which lay somewhere behind the present Woolworths, in
Maidenhead Yard.

We may never know the whole truth about the period predating the
founding of the *burghs* but, in the Anglo-Saxon Chronicle, we have unde-
niable proof that from AD 912–13 onwards Hertford, with its twin *burghs*,
was a place of some importance.

HERTFORD, AD 913–1066

Archaeological evidence for occupation in this period is still limited and
can be summarized as follows.

The Northern *burgh*. Not much evidence and what there is rests to a large
extent on the small amount of late Saxon and Saxo-Norman pottery found
at the Millbridge site. Some fragments of late Stamford Ware (a type of
yellow-glazed pottery often found on late Saxon sites) and a single penny
of William I, found stratified in a deposit above two earlier occupation
layers, the latest of which appears to be a make-up layer possibly contemporary with the construction of the motte and bailey castle.

The Southern *burgh*. Fairly extensive amounts of tenth and eleventh-
century pottery, recovered from excavations at Honey Lane and the Bircherley Green/Railway Street sites. Some evidence for industrial activity in this
period was also recovered. In fact, most of the sites that have been investi-

PLATE 51.   Structural slots and post-holes of a late Saxon building fronting present day
Railway Street, Hertford. During the excavations in 1979 much pottery and
domestic waste was recovered from the large rubbish pits in the yard behind
the building (including the large jug shown on the frontispiece).

PLATE 52. Remains of an early Medieval lime kiln, found during excavations on the site of the old covered market, in Railway Street.

gated, over the area of the Southern *burgh*, have produced at least a little material of tenth-century date (Plates 51 & 52). Distribution of finds in the Southern *burgh* suggests occupation covered the area from the Wash to the line of the large ditch crossing Railway Street. Lack of archaeological investigation is probably the reason for the paucity of evidence from the Fore Street area; no doubt any reasonably comprehensive excavation would, as elsewhere, produce tenth–eleventh-century material. Unfortunately we do not have a large enough body of artefacts or structural elements on which to base a realistic assessment of population numbers, density and type of buildings, or land utilization. There are a couple of sources available to us for filling in part of the picture. The first, Domesday Book, was compiled on the order of William the Conqueror in 1086. This is, in effect, a census and inventory of England from the years after the Conquest. It sets out the taxable value of each and every town, village and hamlet. The Domesday evidence will be discussed in more detail in the next chapter.

THE HERTFORD MINT

The second valuable source is the list of coins minted in Hertford. Sal Garfi in his Survey refers to Aethelstan, the son of Edward the Elder, who became king in AD 925 and the laws he drew up on the minting of coins. Hertford, as a *burgh*, had a mint. We know for certain that minting was carried on in Hertford from at least Aethelstan's reign, by a moneyer called ABONEL and continues until after the Norman Conquest. At times two or more moneyers appear to be striking coins in the same period.

The location of the mint, or mints, are unknown. No trace of coin blanks or coin moulds have so far been discovered. One imagines that the most likely area would be in the Southern *burgh* somewhere probably close to the river.

We have included as Appendix B an article by the late David Fish which gives a fascinating insight into the historical aspects of coin minting in Hertford. Perhaps the most intriguing feature is that 92 per cent of all known coins from the Hertford Mint are in Continental hoards or collections! Even in those days Hertfordshire's money was pouring out to pay Danegeld and St Peter's Pence and ending up in Scandinavia and Rome.

With the rather inconclusive evidence we have to hand at present, it is difficult to say how important Saxon Hertford really was in the tenth century. The Domesday Book does show it to be the county town by the middle of the eleventh century, and comparable in size to many others in the rest of England. This fits quite well with the archaeological evidence, which shows from a number of sites that the amount of pottery and presumably occupation, substantially increases in the Southern *burgh* throughout the tenth and eleventh centuries.

It is reasonable to say that, although the origins of a settlement in Hertford may go back before AD 912, it is from the time of Edward the Elder that Hertford flourishes. It was the years from AD 913 to AD 1042 (the date of Edward the Confessor's accession) which saw the development of the Borough and Royal mint, rising, perhaps from humble beginnings, to become a trading and communications centre for the area north of London and also acting as a defensive outpost protecting the northern limits of the territory of London.

LATE SAXON SETTLEMENT AT WARE

We shall now look at the evidence and attempt to trace the development of Ware from a small, nondescript, Saxon settlement, possibly beginning in the late sixth or seventh century, to the more nucleated but still fairly loosely knit village it must have achieved by the ninth century.

The village must have spanned both sides of the north–south road, which swept down from the low hills to the north to follow the line of present Baldock Street, but continuing on directly south to the river instead of bearing round to the east as today. The first settlement was probably a straggle of huts and cattle enclosures fronting a dusty track meandering northwards away from the river. It is possible that an east–west track along the upper margins of the river terrace was also established at this time but it is doubtful if this amounted to anything more than a riverside trail, or perhaps a trackway out towards the Wareside area – the precursor of the Medieval eastward drift? Much of the above is supposition and is not supported by archaeological evidence. However, in 1984 the Hart Archaeological Unit began a series of excavations between 13-23 Baldock Street. These revealed a series of post-hole and beam slot structures, predating the earliest Medieval houses on the site. At least two phases of these simple wooden buildings were identified and they were on a different alignment to the earliest Medieval frontage which already showed a distinct swing to the east. The earlier wooden buildings were aligned very much north–south, supporting our theory that the Saxon village was based on a north–south plan, with the main north-south street making no deviation to the east but leading directly to the river, where, presumably there was some way of crossing either by way of a ford, a bridge or ferry. The two streams which became known as the Lower and Upper Bournes, would have proved effective territorial boundaries (if not defensive ones) on the east and west sides. The small Saxon church and its holdings would have stood just outside the main village, on the other side of the eastern bourne, alongside the track which headed east along the river (Fig. 14).

Let us try to visualize the situation on the eve of the Conquest. We are standing on a low hill to the north (perhaps somewhere close to where the Fire Station now stands) looking south to the river. We can see wooden huts and buildings lining both sides of probably a broad street. Pens and enclosures for animals lie behind them. Two small streams run down from the low hills forming boundaries on either side of the settlement. St Mary's church – albeit in a much simpler form – lies on the other side of the easternmost stream. Perhaps there are a few scattered buildings along

SAXON & MEDIEVAL

SETTLEMENT

lower bourne

upper bourne

N

Saxon
town

Priory

grounds

Friary
grounds

Medieval   expansion

R.LEA

Roman road (line of)

0   50   100   150   200m.

FIGURE 14.   Plan showing the approximate position of the Saxon and Medieval towns at
Ware; with the position of the Priory and Friary indicated.

the river terrace to the east. Along the riverfront may be crude wharves and
landing stages. Would we also see a bridge? Or possibly more likely a ford
or even a ferry. Was the great park and Lordship, mentioned in Domesday
Book, at Poles on the higher hills to the north? Before us we see a rather
sprawling but thriving settlement, everyone going about their particular
tasks in a reasonably orderly manner. The sturdy buildings and the well

tended herds of goats, pigs and the penned milch cows testify to the hand of a strict but kindly overlord (see Col. Plate VI, p. 94).

Sometime after the Conquest the main street begins to take a decidedly more eastward line. Gradually the direct north–south orientation of the Saxon street becomes of less importance. Now it came down from the low hills to the north and swept round to skirt the southern boundary of St Mary's church and the newly established Alien Priory, to take a line almost at right angles to the old road, heading along the upper reaches of the low gravel terrace parallel with the river. The making of Medieval Ware had begun.

6

The Norman Conquest and Domesday Book

The events and the main protagonists of that fateful year 1066 are very well known to all of us. The after effects on Hertford and the surrounding area must have been traumatic. The year opened with the death, in January, of Edward the Confessor. He had been king of England for twenty-four years. Edward was of the Royal Saxon house and he followed the reigns of two major Scandinavian kings, Cnut and Harthacnut. Edward, although Saxon, had spent part of his earlier life as a Norman monk. French was his natural language and his reign was weak and indecisive. This paved the way for the events of 1066. His pro-Norman policy was challenged by the great Earl Godwin of Wessex, and then by Godwin's son Harold. On Edward's death the lineal descent of the throne was to Edgar the Atheling, an eleven year old boy. However, the English wanted Harold, a strong man, as king. Immediately Harold's right to succeed was challenged by the Norwegian king, Harald Hardrada and by Duke William of Normandy. A power struggle then ensued. Would England revert to Nordic control? Stay Anglo-Saxon? Or come under French control?

All during the summer of 1066 Harold awaited William's attack from Normandy but contrary winds kept William out. Then in September those same winds brought King Hardrada across the North Sea to Yorkshire. Harold moved north to engage and defeat the Norsemen on 28 September in a brilliant victory at Stamford Bridge. Three days later William landed at Pevensey in Sussex. Harold, flushed with victory, led his depleted army south, probably travelling down the old North Road and passing through Ware or Hertford on his way to Hastings, which he reached in four or five days. On 14 October Harold, with a smallish body of largely exhausted troops and unwisely without waiting for reinforcements, opposed William. At Hastings William secured a narrow victory with a force of some 10,000–12,000 troops of which about 5,000 were mounted knights. These knights proved to be the deciding factor in what was a very close run thing. He dared not march to beseige London immediately, because it was still strongly defended. Instead he crossed the Thames at Wallingford and moved west and north of London into Buckinghamshire and Hertfordshire, thereby cutting London off from obtaining reinforcements from the north and west.

Harold had held extensive estates in our area. Waltham Abbey was one of his great churches. He was well known locally and no doubt many from Hertfordshire fought and died with him at Stamford Bridge and Hastings. This may account for the severe way William dealt with our area, pillaging and brutally ravaging our shire until London surrendered. Harold's estates and those of his followers in Hertfordshire and the surrounding area were pillaged and laid waste in what must have been a terrible autumn for the local people. William and his army were probably originally based at Berkhamsted but he would have made sure of securing all the important towns and route centres, including Hertford. The surrender finally took place at Berkhamsted. William was crowned king in London at Christmas 1066.

Domesday Book graphically tells the story. It gives the value of various estates before 1066, then the value when the Norman overlords took over in 1067 and again in 1086. Towns like Hertford and Ware appear to have escaped fairly lightly, maybe they surrendered quickly; but in contrast look at the value of some country holdings before and after 1066:

	pre-1066	post-1066	1086
Amwell	£18	£12	£14 10s 0d
Codecote	£5	£2	£2
Hertingfordbury	£10	£6	£8
Stanstead	£20	£10	£17
Bengeo (part)	£8	£3	£5
Hoddesdon (part)	£30	£22	£24
Hailey	£4	£0 10s 0d	£1 10s 0d
Brickendon (part)	£8	£5	£5
Panshanger	£2	£0 15s 0d	£0 15s 0d

Whereas the figures for Hertford and Ware are:

Hertford	£7 10s 0d	£15	£20
Ware	£50	£45	£50

(NB. The Hertford amount was not its true value but rather the amount the *burgh* paid the Crown for the right to trade.)

What this must have meant in human terms is apparent too. The value of an estate depended on the male workers. Land was only of value if it could be ploughed; without a ploughman and his oxen it lost its value. In the villages the values fell by about 50 per cent in a year. The male population may also have declined by about that figure: presumably not all were killed, but a mortality of one in four or five of the country workers is not an unreasonable assumption. The women and children most likely fared little better.

The Normans were highly organized and their *modus operandi* for the subjection of England, if there was any resistance, was to devastate the countryside and then set up motte and bailey castles as fortified bases for their knights and men at arms. These mottes were large mounds of earth fortified and ditched all round, with flat open areas, or baileys, in front. On the motte there would have been a wooden palisaded tower. The whole thing was rather like the layout of a masonry castle, but built in earth and timber.

In that October of 1066 William would probably have kept the main body of his army at Berkhamsted, to guard against any attempt to relieve London from the north or west. Parts of his force would have been detached to take over important centres and to fortify them. One of these was Hertford. A force of say 100 knights with men at arms would have been quite enough to do that. We can imagine the consternation and panic with their arrival at Hertford and the burgesses assessing their chances. Tales of pillage, rape and burning would already have reached them as also, probably, had refugees. They would have no choice but a quick surrender and co-operation with the invaders. One can imagine the town notables desperately seeking a French speaker, perhaps a priest or trader, to present their case and smooth the handing over to the Norman leader. They would undoubtedly have been ordered to provide food, shelter, home comforts and services to the Normans. The first major act of the new overlords would have been the construction of a motte and bailey castle, with the resulting impressment of the local population to provide labour to build it (see Col. Plate VIII, p. 130).

We, of course, know the site they chose for the motte, it still stands today on the south bank of the Lea close to the ford, in a corner of the later castle grounds. It was ideally situated for controlling the ford and dominating the Southern *burgh*. The mound today is a shadow of the original construction, which must have been at least twice as high and much wider. The river Lea flowed past it on the north side and a moat, leading from the river, surrounded it on the other sides. The bailey was probably to the south and south-west and would also have been surrounded by a deep ditch and bank. The motte would have towered with massive authority above the town below. One can imagine work gangs of Hertford's citizens digging the moats and piling high the resulting earth to form the motte. Trees felled and a constant procession of tree trunks and logs being hauled and trimmed for the wooden fortifications, both on top of the motte and on the crests of the banks around the bailey.

The Normans would be out each day, with accompanying strings of packhorses and carts, gathering supplies from the surrounding countryside and putting the torch to any villages which resisted. Anyone who protested or refused would have been killed on the spot. Any other able bodied men, women and children would have been brought back to work for them as slaves. By Christmas William was crowned king and he rewarded his loyal knights by allotting them lands formerly owned by the Saxon Thanes. When the Norman overlords took possession of their holdings the pillaging would have been stopped, as they restored and jealously guarded their new estates.

One of William's first acts was to appoint a King's Officer for each Shire, ostensibly to keep order but also as a counterweight to his aspiring barons. Peter de Valognes was appointed Sheriff of Hertfordshire and it was he who took over the guardianship of the castle at Hertford. In fact, he might well have been personally involved in the building of it in AD 1066-7. However, though master of the castle, Hertford town was not his possession, it still remained a *Burgus* and no one's personal property except the king's.

According to Domesday Book, before 1066 Ware was owned by one Askell of Ware. He must have been a wealthy man as he owned land north of Ware as well as Westmill, Sacombe, and the Pelhams. Domesday's valuation of Ware is £50 before 1066 and £45 in 1067; hardly changed in contrast to many surrounding estates. Like Hertford, Ware seems not to have suffered much at the hands of the Normans. Maybe Askell had been killed fighting alongside Harold at Stamford Bridge or Hastings and Ware, being then leaderless, surrendered quickly without resistance. Certainly, one would think it must have been occupied and garrisoned but no castle or other fortifications appear to have been deemed necessary.

DOMESDAY BOOK

Before looking more closely at the Domesday Book it is useful to understand why, when and how it was compiled. After Hastings William treated England as if the whole of it was his own property. He parcelled out the lands of England to his followers on personal whims. The Church estates were confirmed, usually under Norman appointees; the Saxon *burghs* were retained by the king. The Domesday Survey was commissioned by William, to find out how much each landholder held – land, livestock, workers and the value of such. A massive inventory of property, compiled county by county; but within each county it is listed landowner by landowner, not by area.

For example, to find out what Bengeo was like you have to add together the entries from all the different landowners. The exception to this in our area is the Borough of Hertford which has an entry all of its own. As a Royal Borough it was not owned by anyone else although certain people

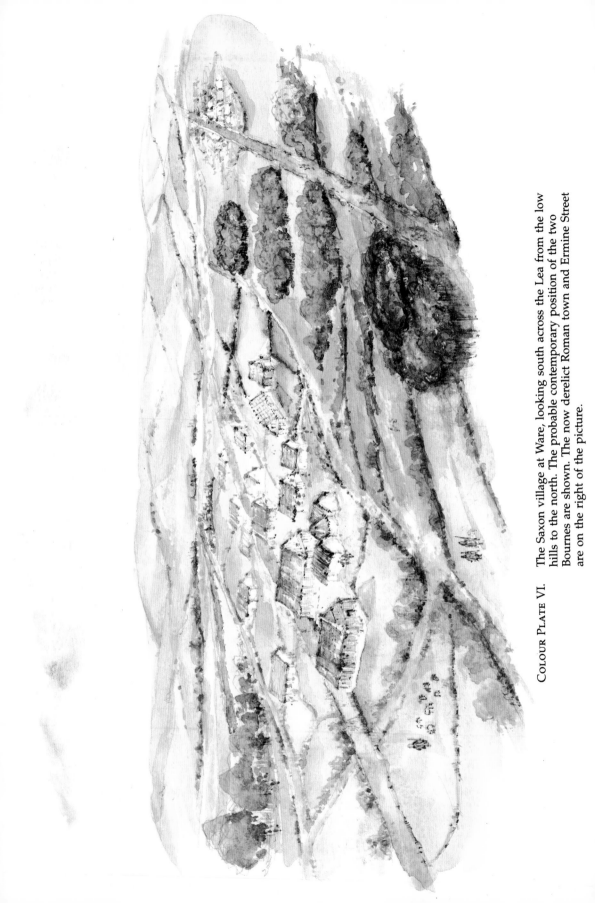

COLOUR PLATE VI.   The Saxon village at Ware, looking south across the Lea from the low hills to the north. The probable contemporary position of the two Bournes are shown. The now derelict Roman town and Ermine Street are on the right of the picture.

owned individual houses or rented them from the Crown. Other towns in Hertfordshire are not listed in this way but are shown under the names of the individual landowners. For example, Ware was owned by Hugh de Grantmesnil and is shown under his name. St Albans was owned by St Albans Abbey and is one of their many holdings.

The entry for Hertford reads thus:

The Borough of HERTFORD
1. answered for 10 hides before 1066, but does not now do so. There were 146 burgesses in King Edward's jurisdiction.
2. Of these Count Alan now has 3 houses which paid dues then and now.
3. Eudo the Steward has 2 houses which were Algar of Cokenach's, which paid dues then and now; Eudo also has a third house, which was Wulfmer of Eton's, which does not pay its dues.
4. Geoffrey of Bec, 3 houses which pay dues.
5. Humphrey of Anneville holds 2 houses with one garden under Eudo. One of these was leased to a Reeve of the king's; the other, with its garden, was a burgess's, and now the burgesses claim them back, as wrongfully taken from them.
6. King William has another 18 burgesses who were Earl Harold's and Earl Leofwin's men, who pay all dues.
7. Peter of Valognes has 2 churches with 1 house, which he bought from Wulfwy of Hatfield, which pay all dues. Wulfwy could grant and sell them.
8. Geoffrey de Mandeville has some premises which were Asgar the Constable's and 7 houses which paid no dues except the king's tax, when it was collected.
9. Ralph Baynard has 2 houses which paid dues then and now.
10. Hardwin of Scales has 14 houses which Aki had; before 1066 they gave no dues except the king's tax. Hardwin cited the king as protector for them. Further, Hardwin has one house by the king's gift, which was a burgess's, which pays all dues.
11. This borough town pays £20, assayed and weighed, and 3 mills pay £10 at face value; when Peter the Sheriff acquired it it paid £15 at face value; before 1066 £7.10s at face value.

Ten hides is an area about one mile wide and two miles long. (A hide was a variable area of a piece of land that would support one household. In this part of the country it was around 120 acres.) An area of ten hides is much larger than the area of the twin *burghs*. The Domesday Book distinguishes in line one between *Burgus*, i.e. the garrisoned fortress, and *Suburbium*, translated in paragraph 11 as 'borough town'. The ten hides must refer to the latter which would be made up of the original *burghs* (the garrisoned area), plus an area of surrounding land. Where then was this land? It did not include Bengeo, Sele, Hertingfordbury, Brickendon (Horns Mill), Epcombs, Amwell or Hailey as all these are separately mentioned in Domesday. It could have included Hartham and the Meads between Hertford and Ware and an area south-east and south of the town, that may have included land south of the River Beane on its north side, with a western boundary halfway to Epcombs and Hertingfordbury, including the present Hospital area, then to the south including West Street and the higher ground around County Hall and part of Balls Park and Foxholes Farm: then running north to the Meads somewhere close to where the A10 Viaduct now crosses.

Presumably at least some of the burgesses were the descendants of the original garrison of the twin *burghs* from AD 912/13. They were freemen, owning their own houses, or holding them as of right from the king. They must also have been involved with and responsible for regulating the trade and commerce of the town, looking after the interests of the other townsfolk and controlling the Market. Some of the burgesses' houses must have been taken from them after the Conquest (see entries No. 5 and No. 10).

We know that by the time of Edward the Confessor there were 146 burgesses living and trading in Hertford. They would have had families, servants, retainers and workmen. So if we assess them at seven per burgess, we have a population of, say, 900 persons. But it is doubtful if this gives a fair indication of the town's population. No doubt there were other inhabitants, apart from burgesses, who did not have rights and privileges and are not noted in Domesday Book. These other inhabitants would have had their families and dependants and this might well double the figure to a more realistic population of around 2,000 in all. The number of houses mentioned in the Domesday entry is 54, so perhaps 92 were still owned by the original burgesses who are not named.

In paragraph 7 it states that Peter de Valognes has two churches. There is no other mention of churches in the borough in the Domesday Book. At that time one presumes that St Mary-the-Less at Old Cross and St Nicolas at the back of Maidenhead Street were in existence and also All Saints. St Andrews is almost certainly a later addition. Peter de Valognes was the Sheriff of the County and clearly a man of stature. So why was one church withheld from his overlordship? It may have had something to do with the fact that one of the churches was on the north side of the river. It may be that the two churches 'owned' by him were the two on the south side of the river – St Nicholas and All Saints. St Mary's may have been owned by someone else or may have formed part of a separate holding which included most, if not all, of the Northern *burgh*. We have already suggested that the Northern *burgh* may never have been as important as the Southern *burgh*. Perhaps by 1066 it had become even more run down and was not thought to be of sufficient worth to warrant dividing up. It may be that it was more or less left to its own devices as long as the necessary dues were paid.

We know that there were three mills in the town. One, the town mill, may have been just upstream of the ford. The mills at Sele and Epcombs are separately mentioned and were not owned by the town. Neither was

Horns Mill which belonged to Brickendon. Dicker Mill might have been a possibility for one of the other mills but it does not appear to have existed before the late twelfth century. One possible explanation is that all three mills mentioned were in the town centre just above the Wash. Perhaps there was just one large mill complex with three separate sets of millstones worked by different families.

The statement that the *Suburbium*, or borough town, pays £20 seems a relatively modest sum and before 1066 it was only £7 10s! Ware in contrast had a value of £50 before 1066. But it may be that Hertford did not pay its full value for some reason or other. The trouble with Domesday Book is that when it comes to deal with a borough like Hertford the entries bearing on its wealth and population are short and limited. For example, if we compare the entry for a village, say, Hertingfordbury which belonged to Ralph Baynard, the entry is much more detailed.

[In HERTFORD Hundred]
Ralph holds HERTINGFORDBURY himself. It answers for 5 hides. Land for 10 ploughs. In lordship 3 hides and 1 virgate. 2 ploughs there; a third possible. 5 villagers with 1 Frenchman and 6 smallholders have 5 ploughs; a further 2 possible. 11 cottagers; 4 slaves.
2 mills at 6s; meadow for 3 ploughs; pasture for the village livestock; woodland, 200 pigs; from woodland and pasture 7s. Total value £8; when acquired £6; before 1066 £10. Alwin, a thane of Earl Harold's held this manor; he could sell.

As can be seen the population and resources of the village are dealt with more comprehensively and all this adds up to 26 households, perhaps around 100 people.

Bengeo is an interesting one as there are quite a number of landowners.

Count Alan	1 Virgate	2 Households
1 Frenchman	½ Virgate	1 Household
Peter de Valognes	½ Virgate	1 Household

and three large ones as follows:

Hugh de Beauchamp's Manor
6 hides (700 acres as one Manor). 2 men at arms, 8 ploughs, 7 villagers, 6 smallholders, 2 slaves, 1 mill, meadow for 3 ploughs, pasture, woodland, 20 pigs.

Geoffrey de Mandeville's Manor
Howard holds 3 hides and 1 virgate, 400 acres from Geoffrey as a Manor with 4 ploughs, 3 villagers, 2 smallholders, 6 cottagers, 1 mill, meadow for 1 plough, pasture, woodland, 4 pigs.

Geoffrey de Bec Manors and Land
Geoffrey holds 5 hides and 1 virgate (600 acres) as one manor, land for 5 ploughs, 2 Frenchmen, 2 villagers, 6 smallholders, 34 cottagers, meadow for 2 ploughs, pasture

for livestock, wood for fences. In the same village 6½ hides (750 acres) as one manor, 8 ploughs, 4 men at arms, 2 villagers, 10 smallholders, 5 slaves, meadow pasture, woodland, 30 pigs.

In the same village 3 men at arms hold 1 hide and 1½ virgates (200 acres).

In the same village Roger holds 5½ virgates.

In the same village a priest and a Frenchman hold 3½ virgates from Geoffrey.

Putting all these holdings together they comprise, at least, some 3,000 acres of land, and some 105 households, probably a population of around 500–600 people. A large holding, but of course it may have been fairly scattered with the four manors spread well apart. (Geoffrey de Mandeville also owned Sele which was ½ hide with 2 slaves and a mill.) Was the priest mentioned for St Leonard's? The two mills mentioned were possibly one at Molewood, on the Beane, and the other somewhere on the Rib, or at Stapleford.

Bengeo was obviously quite a large estate and would have extended well to the north and probably included Waterford and Stapleford, then eastward to include Stonyhills, Chapmore End and Tonwell, then along the Rib towards Wadesmill.

The Domesday Book entry for Ware is:

[In BRAUGHING Hundred]
Hugh of Grantmesnil holds 24 hides in WARE. Land for 38 ploughs. In lordship 13 hides; 3 ploughs there; another 3 possible. 38 villagers with a priest and the village Reeve, and with 3 Frenchmen and 2 Englishmen, have 26½ ploughs; (a further 5½ ploughs possible); 27 smallholders; 12 cottagers; 9 slaves. Under the Frenchmen and Englishmen are 32 men of the villagers and smallholders. 2 mills at 24s, and 400 eels less 25; the other men have 3 mills which pay 10s a year; meadow for 20 ploughs; woodland, 400 pigs. A park for woodland beasts; 4 arpents of vines, just planted.
    Total value £45; when acquired £50; before 1066 as much.
    Askell of Ware held this manor, and 1 Freeman, his man, had 2 hides. Another Freeman, Earl Gyrth's man, held ½ hide; both could sell. These were placed in this manor after 1066; they did not belong here before 1066, as the Shire testifies.

It shows a substantial settlement with extensive estates. Hugh de Grantmesnil alone held 24 hides, or nearly 3,000 acres of fertile land, sustaining 38 ploughs. The valuation of £50 was a considerable sum in those days.

This entry for Ware in Domesday seems to describe not so much an urban town like Hertford, but a rather more village-like settlement set within prosperous estates, perhaps not unlike Bengeo but larger and possibly more formal. Unlike Hertford, Berkhamsted and St Albans, Ware had no burgesses nor any merchants like Cheshunt. The extent of the Ware estates can be traced by looking at the position of those surrounding it. We have Hadham and Widford held by the Bishop of London, Hunsdon, Stanstead Abbotts, Amwell, Hertford, and Bengeo. To the north was Thundridge and this was rented by Hugh de Grantmesnil, from the Bishop of Bayeux. Perhaps the Ware holdings are in the wedge-shaped area ranging from the Rib to the west, then north and east towards Wadesmill, east towards the Hadhams and south to the Ash. This takes in the village of Wareside and the hamlets of Butlers Green, Babbs Green, Nobland Green, Blakesware, Mardocks Mill, Newhall Green, Westmill, Fanhams and Reeves Green. The latter place is interesting – could this have been where the Reeve of Ware lived? The Reeve, the village policeman, was there to keep order and see fair play. The Domesday entry describes about 125 houses. Maybe a large proportion of these households were in the vill of Ware itself. The Priest must have been at St Mary's, which seems to confirm its foundation as a Saxon church (see below).

Peter Walne, former County Archivist, comments:

My extensive searches for possible documentation before 1066, of a church in Ware, have not produced much of relevance. The best information that I have been able to find is a charter of William I, dated 1081 at Winchester. It confirms many grants of properties in England, by a number of land owners, to the Abbey of St Evroul in Normandy. The immediately relevant matter is the mention of the grant by Hugo de Grantmesnil, Lord of the Manor of Ware, of the church of Ware together with the titles attached thereto, along with two carucates of land. Included in this grant was the church at Thundridge and its tithes, since Thundridge was a chapel of Ware. No text of Hugo's grant is known in England or France. Since, however the facts of Hugo's grant is amongst those confirmed in 1081, this is the earliest reference to a church in Ware and antedates the Domesday Survey and the resulting Domesday Book.

This 1081 reference and the mention of a priest in the account of Ware in Domesday Book is reasonably circumstantial evidence of a church which must have existed in 1066 and before. Edith Hunt's reference in her *History of Ware* to 1078 as the date of Hugo's grant is the result of a misunderstanding of the figure 1078 at the top of a page in Volume VI, part 2 of the much expanded 1830 edition of Sir William Dugdale's *Monasticon Anglicanum*, on which page and the next, the text of William's Charter of 1081 occurs. She mistook page number for year date.

The best text of this charter is in Book VI of Ordericus Vitalis, *Historia Anglicanum* in the edition by Auguste le Prevost, a French scholar (Vol. III, 1855).

There are no less than five mills mentioned for Ware in Domesday Book. Possibly two or three of these were on the Lea at Ware, maybe one at Wadesmill and one somewhere along the Ash, probably at Mardocks. Plenty of woodland, a park to the north of Ware village and a vineyard on the slopes above the village and lots of eels.

Before leaving Domesday it is interesting to compare Hertford and Ware with other towns or villages in the County.

Hertford	146 burgesses
Ware	125 households, no burgesses
St Albans	80 households, including 46 burgesses
Berkhamsted	91 households, including 52 burgesses
Bishop's Stortford	27 households, no burgesses
Hitchin	92 households, no burgesses
Cheshunt	63 households, including 10 merchants but no burgesses

And also compare them with other major towns:

Exeter	315 households
Canterbury	262 households
Warwick	225 households
Norwich	738 households
Northampton	60 households

Hertford was therefore not insignificant on a national scale and certainly, going on the number of burgesses, the most important town in the County. Ware was an estate of considerable value and a settlement of comparable size to Hitchin, Berkhamsted and St Albans. The Domesday Book does not list any burgesses for Ware but it does list mills, workers and extensive lands.

7
To Middle Age

The last chapter of this book deals with events from AD 1066 to around AD 1266. This period is documented history and as it is dealt with fairly comprehensively in various other histories of the two towns it is not our intention here to reiterate much of what has already been chronicled. We are, however, concerned with certain events of these years to the extent which they affect the status, layout and development of the two towns.

This part of the story can really be summed up under four headings: (1) The Royal Castle at Hertford. (2) Bridges at Ware. (3) Religious Houses in the towns. (4) Expansion of Trade and Commerce in the towns. Before we consider these in more detail it might be helpful to provide some background to each.

Castles In the years immediately following the Norman invasion many motte and bailey castles were hastily thrown up. They were built for the sole purpose of dominating the populace and thus securing the countryside. In many cases they were soon replaced by larger, more sophisticated earthworks. Later on many were reconstructed in stone with tall keeps and the massive curtain walls which are often depicted in storybooks. They were both dwellings for the Norman overlords and military barracks. These stone castles were impregnable fortresses and unless they were either battered into submission by seige engines, or starved out, the occupants were usually quite safe from attack.

During times of trouble and strife, such as the civil war between Stephen and Matilda in the early twelfth century, the local barons in their castles became virtually independent of royal control. When a strong king came to the throne, such as Henry Plantaganet (Henry II) he decided that the barons' power should be curbed. Many castles were sequestered and permission to build and castellate new ones had to be obtained from the king – a sort of royal planning permission!

The Ware Bridges We have already seen that when there was a bridge in existence at Ware, the main route from London to the north went through the town. At Hertford the ford was then little used except for local access. In post-Roman times, after the bridge fell into disrepair, Hertford flourished. So for the sake of our story it is important to try and discover, if we can, where and when the later bridges were built at Ware. Bridges are not mentioned in Domesday Book nor the Anglo-Saxon Chronicle. This could mean that none existed or they were considered of such little consequence that they weren't recorded.

Religious Houses It is difficult for us today to envisage the enormous power of the Church in this period. It is ironic that the Normans, a warlike and aggressive people, were extremely pious and great supporters of the Church. The Pope himself had blessed William's expedition in 1066. Bishops, and church leaders, such as the Battling Bishop Odo of Bayeux, William's half-brother, fought alongside other knights in William's army. William's legality and power was based on the legitimacy of his coronation by the Church. In return he and his followers wholeheartedly supported the Church. Two of these followers, who were granted lands in our area, were typical of this.

The first was Ralph de Limesi, one of William's foremost knights, who took over the lands of Amwell. As pious Normans, he and his wife founded and endowed the Priory at Hertford, which originally had extensive holdings on the eastern edge of the town, in the area occupied today by Priory Street and Railway Street (see Fig. 13, p. 80).

The second was Hugh de Grantmesnil, who was awarded the lands of Ware. In 1081 he is recorded as granting the Church at Ware (St Mary's), plus substantial land, to the Abbey of St Evroul (in Normandy) to establish the Benedictine Priory at Ware as an Alien cell.

Much later on, at the end of the fourteenth century, another endowment by Thomas Lord Wake led to the establishment of a house of the Friars Minor (Franciscans) at Ware (the surviving buildings of which are very confusingly now known as the Priory).

Trade and Commerce Whatever one thinks of the Normans they, in their day, were the most dynamic and energetic race in Europe and William was one of the most able men of his time. The Normans' influence expanded to take in other parts of France, Spain, North Africa, Naples and Sicily. At the time of the first crusade, they took over Antioch and reached Jerusalem itself. Like their Viking forebears the Normans were great traders and encouraged reciprocal trade. William knew the advantages of towns. He used them both to encourage trade and as a counterbalance to the power of the feudal barons in the countryside.

HERTFORD

The Royal Castle

The original Norman motte and bailey castle was under the guardianship of Peter de Valognes, Sheriff of Hertfordshire and Essex. The guardianship eventually passed to his son Roger, who appears to have been a supporter of the Empress Matilda in her civil war with King Stephen. Matilda's son, Henry Plantagenet finally succeeded Stephen and was crowned Henry II in 1154. He, as has already been mentioned, annexed castles from some of the barons. He improved many of them and strengthened them against attack by the rogue barons.

It was Henry who was responsible for rebuilding the castle at Hertford, between AD 1170 and 1175. We can still see the largely surviving stone and flint curtain walls. Originally it was surrounded by a double moat. A section of this moat, on the south side of the Wash, was excavated by Martin Petchey for Hertford Museum, with the help of the Hart Archaeological Unit, in advance of the construction of Castle Hall. The excavations revealed a massively deep inner moat and a not so deep outer section. The present road pattern of Castle Street, Parliament Square, and the Wash was established to accommodate the circuit of this double moat. The western side of the moat turned to join with the River Lea, passing immediately in front of the present building known as the castle. The central part of this building was originally a brick-built gate house, erected by Edward IV *c.* 1463–5.

It was, therefore, Henry's castle that dictated the layout of the streets on the western side of the town. There probably was expansion along what is now West Street, where some village-like ribbon development was established. The south-west postern gate of the castle, which still survives, served to give access to this area from the twelfth or thirteenth centuries onwards. These are the Plan Units in Sal Garfi's survey numbered 7, 9, and 10 (see Fig. 13, p. 80). In Castle Street, on what was the old Express Dairy site before the present office development was built, the Hertfordshire Archaeological Trust carried out an excavation across the line of the double moat. These excavations revealed that the line of the double moat was turning towards the river at that point. On a bank between the moats they found evidence of some masonry structure. This was thought to be contemporary with the main period of castle building and possibly was to do with some outer bailey or defence work of Henry's time.

The Priory and Churches

Sometime after AD 1066 Ralph de Limesi took over the manor of Amwell. His holdings also included land on the east side of the borough of Hertford; the area of Priory Street, Railway Street, the present Hertford East Station and the old Christ's Hospital site. It may well be that before 1066 some of this land had belonged to the borough of Hertford. Ralph was a typically pious Norman and he made a grant of land (one hide) for the construction of a Priory at Hertford. He and his wife both endowed it with other property. The Priory Church was built between present day Priory Street and St John's Street. An area that was latterly occupied by Jewson's timber yard but is now the new residential complex Mitre Court. The site now lies close to the River Lea which, in those days, flowed further to the north. The Priory lands also included the area now known as Dicker Mills. The site of the Priory Church was investigated by the Hertfordshire Archaeological Trust in 1990, before Mitre Court was built. The foundations of the church were located but had been badly knocked about and damaged by the pilfering

PLATE 53.   One of the burials discovered during excavations on the site of Hertford Priory.

of stone when the Priory went out of use. Numerous graves were also uncovered, dating to when the Priory was in use (Plate 53). This Priory, a cell of the Abbey of St Albans, was quite a small one with, it is said, only about six brothers. Ralph de Limesi himself eventually became its Prior, his wife a sister and they were both buried there.

Excavations by the Hart Archaeological Unit at Bircherley Green in 1980, on the line of the ditch of the Saxon *burgh*, showed that the ditch was deliberately backfilled in the late eleventh or early twelfth century. This filling of the ditch may well have been contemporary with the founding of the Priory. The original Saxon defences had, in any case, been made redundant by the building of the Castle. At this time Fore Street may also have been extended eastwards, therefore straddling the line of the former Saxon ditch down which the Ashbourne stream originally flowed.

By about AD 1200 the layout of the town centre was set and really there was little change until the eighteenth and nineteenth centuries. Despite some piecemeal development and the clearance and subsequent infilling of the town centre the original thirteenth-century street plan is still very much with us today.

In the Old Cross–St Andrew Street area it is likely that the banks and ditches of the Northern *burgh* were also levelled and filled in by the twelfth century, thus allowing the development of St Andrew Street to continue unhindered westward of Brewhouse Lane (Garfi's Plan Unit 4).

The dating of St Andrews Church is fairly crucial to our arguments in this area. The late Canon R. H. Gill, who was rector of St Andrews parish from 1952 to 1970, in his booklet *The Parish Church of Hertford, St. Andrew*, published in 1957 quotes a number of authorities to support his view that St Andrews was Hertford's first church and was founded in AD 860 i.e. before the Northern *burgh* was built. As we have suggested earlier it is possible that St Andrews was within the Northern *burgh* and could have formed part of the defensive layout of AD 912. However we have no real evidence for this and we believe that the church of St Mary-the-Less at Old Cross is more likely to have been the earlier Saxon church.

Canon Gill lists the first rector of St Andrews as Adam of Essex, installed in AD 1207 by the Bishop of Lincoln. We should therefore be safe in assuming a church on that site by the early thirteenth century, if not earlier.

Before moving on we ought perhaps to fill out our narrative with some observations on Bengeo and the problem of Hertingfordbury.

Bengeo and St Leonard's

The name Bengeo (Beaninghoh) is English and means something like 'The spur of the dwellers by the Beane'. Therefore I think we can accept that there was some English or Saxon settlement there. The obvious place is on or somewhere close to the elevated spur of land by St Leonard's church, which does overlook the Beane.

As Hertford developed and more traffic used Port Hill, no doubt the village expanded, ribbon development taking place along the road leading north to Wadesmill and the Ermine Street.

The Domesday Book entry for Bengeo gives four manors, those of Hugh de Beauchamp, Geoffrey de Mandeville and Geoffrey de Bec. Geoffrey de Bec's holding is described as being two manors in the same village and the village is the only entry with a priest. It seems likely that the priest was at St Leonard's. The church is very Saxon-like architecturally, but was probably built in the early Norman period. The following notes were supplied by the Rev. Colin Weale.

The little Norman church of St Leonard was probably at the heart of the ancient village of Bengeo. In the past, as today, scribes had trouble in spelling the word. The Institution records of the Bishops of Lincoln (Bengeo was in the ancient diocese of Lincoln until the nineteenth century) provide a number of different spellings during the thirteenth century fron Beningho, Beninghou, Beninchho, Beneygho to the Benag in a papal letter!

The little church, it is believed, occupied the site of a much earlier church. Probably the original was made of wattle and daub. When the Danes ravaged the district of Hertford and Ware it probably met the fate of all the other churches and houses in the area. It is thought that the present simple Norman structure replaced the old Saxon church, possibly incorporating some of its features, and was built about AD 1120. The oldest parts are the south door and the chancel arch. Local craftsmen were used in the building of these churches, and would very likely have used their Saxon skills under Norman direction.

The early records are flimsy, so that we cannot say with any certainty who financed the building of the church. The Domesday survey shows that the Norman overlords were Geoffrey de Bec and Hugh de Beauchamp who held almost the whole of Bengeo between them (i.e. 2,565 out of 3,000 acres). The late Herbert Andrews was of the opinion that while the priest mentioned in the Domesday survey for Bengeo cultivated land held of Geoffrey de Bec, he was responsible to Hugh de Beauchamp, lord of the manor.

Under these Norman overlords were several other important sub-tenants, namely, the Engaynes, de Tanys and Fitz Simons. In 1156, it is recorded in the Chronicle for the Priory of Bermondsey that Reginald de Tany gave the advowson (i.e. the right of presentation and ownership) of the church of Bengeo to them. Evidently, at some time the overlordship of the land and the church passed from Hugh de Beauchamp to the de Tany family. They in turn endowed the monks of Bermondsey with the church. This meant that the monastery would hold the rectorial tithes and would have to appoint a vicar to carry out the work of ministry in the parish.

The Priory at Bermondsey was a Clunaic foundation, having its origins in France as an offshoot of La Charité-sur-Loire. It was founded here by an

Englishman Alwin Child, of London, between 1082 and 1089. William Rufus gave the monks land at Bermondsey and this, together with its situation in view of the city of London, attracted many rich benefactors, among whom were the de Tanys. Their gift to the Priory was confirmed in 1272. In that year Reginald and Richard de Tany also gave to the monks of St Saviour's, Bermondsey, the manor of Bengeo which was called 'Richmond' (a small property of some 30 acres in 1086) north of Bengeo. The custom of making gifts of lands and churches to monasteries was encouraged. As one writer puts it, 'they [i.e. the monks] were *'pauperes Christi'* [Christ's poor] and needed the money for their work.' Sadly, as the years went by, they themselves often became Christ's rich.

Vicars, that is substitutes, since monks with their vows of stability were not allowed to be parish priests with a cure of souls, were employed by their monastic patrons to look after the churches. They were very poorly paid and often employed on an *ad hoc* basis. Although we have no record of the names of the early vicars who served Bengeo church before 1245, we do know how much they received as a stipend. The amount was about one third of the profits of the benefice, derived from altar dues, tithes and glebe land. A house was often provided.

In Bishop Hugh's (Bishop of Lincoln 1209–35) register of the ordination of vicarages written *c.* 1218, commonly called the *Liber Antiquus*, it is recorded: 'The vicarage in the church of Bengeo which belongs to the Priory of Bermondsey, ordained a long time ago, consists of all the lesser tithes and offerings of the altar. The vicar bears all ordinary burdens except the provision of hospitality for the archdeacon [i.e. when on visitation] for which the prior is responsible. However, the vicar pays one bezant [gold piece] annually to the said prior which is due and ancient . . .'

This is the stipend which William de Burgh would have received in 1245. He was chaplain to Cardinal John of Toledo and on 15 June 1245 the Pope allowed him to hold the vicarage of Bengeo, besides two others which he already had (*Cal. Papal Letters* i, 217). He was vicar for just six years, and probably never resided, but put a curate in his place.

It remained a vicarage until the nineteenth century, when in 1848 Mr Abel Smith of Woodhall Park, who had purchased the rectorial tithes in 1846, turned the living into a rectory. The Abel Smith family remain patrons of the living to this day.

(Rev. C. A. Weale, Caister-on-Sea, 1994.)

Hertingfordbury

At Hertingfordbury we have an intriguing situation. The old name for Hertingfordbury (Hertfordingebur) means 'the stronghold of the people of Hertford'. This description is somewhat puzzling as by no stretch of the imagination could Hertingfordbury be equated with the Northern *burgh* of Hertford. If not a *burgh* what then could the name be referring to? The late Ken Rutherford-Davis did suggest that there could have been some sort of defended, perhaps even moated, site there in the period before AD 912. This could have been used as a refuge or redoubt for Hertfordians in times of trouble. Whatever the truth of the matter, Domesday Book does not speak of a fort or stronghold here, merely a Lordship of three hides.

Development of Trade and Commerce

After the conquest William wanted his new possessions to be prosperous and produce him revenue and taxes. He recognized the advantages of continuing the rights and privileges of the Saxon towns, the *burghs* like Hertford. He invested them with local burgesses and appointed a bailiff to collect the royal dues. The bailiff and his burgesses, or corporation, had wide powers to fix market dues, charges and tolls for bridges and fords. For example, Hertford's bailiff was not only responsible for fixing tolls in Hertford but also the control of trade and the bridge at Ware. He was empowered to close that bridge unless tolls were paid. When the Wareites rebelled and rid themselves of the bailiff of Hertford Ware began to prosper once again in its own right.

It was William who laid the foundation for the running of the Borough with a Mayor and Corporation, a system which was respected by later monarchs. Hertford as a royal borough began to expand. It was probably about this time that the original ditches of the Saxon *burgh* became redundant; as the town prospered it grew and spread over and beyond the circuit of the earlier defences (see Fig. 15, p. 122).

WARE

The Priory and Friary

At Ware the earliest reference to the foundation of a religious house is of a Benedictine Priory, founded as an Alien cell in the eleventh century on land north of St Mary's Church which was granted to the Abbey of St Evroul by Hugh de Grantmesnil in 1081. We do not know what the people of Ware felt when their parish church was granted to an Alien Priory, but it took them until 1231, 170 years, to get their vicar back. Excavations by the Hart Archaeological Unit in the gardens of the present Manor House, said to be on the site of the Alien Benedictine Priory, revealed some fragments of structural evidence. These could have been the remains of part of a cloister or walkway. Such evidence as we have, which is fairly slim, does suggest that the Priory probably did exist in this area.

PLATE 54. In 1977, at Ware Priory, the trench for new sewer pipes cut right through the remains of the original Friary church. In the photograph the north wall is at the bottom and the south wall near the top; between them can be seen the rammed chalk floors of at least two phases of building.

The other major religious establishment was the Friary (now popularly known as the Priory). It was a cell of the Friars Minor (Franciscans) and was founded in 1338, possibly on partly made-up land reclaimed from the river margins. Rescue excavations during sewerage pipe works revealed the walls and floors of a building just to the north-east of the existing standing buildings. This is believed to be the site of the Friary Church (Plate 54). More recently major refit work has allowed a closer, more intimate look at some of the hitherto inaccessible areas. Tom McDonald, Field Officer for the Hertfordshire Archaeological Trust, has been closely monitoring the work and has recorded more, and in some cases, new evidence for the layout and structural phases of the main Friary building and the cloisters. See also the remarks in Appendix C.

Bridges and Fords

Post-1066 Ware had none of Hertford's advantages as a Royal Borough but it did have one priceless asset – its bridges carrying the major north–south highway, originally established by the Romans. The problem of defining the exact crossing place of any bridge, at any particular time, is a vexed one.

We know from various sources that there were bridges at Ware, or at least in the parish of Ware, from as early as Roman times. The Roman bridge, though the oldest, is the easiest to pinpoint. We know where the Roman road crossed the Meads on the south side of the river – the causeway is still plainly visible today (see Plate 10, p. 31). We also know the line of the road on the north side of the river where it passes through the Glaxo site and then on northwards to Puckeridge. Any bridge must have been just east of the present Lock. A bridge would have been in existence from the earliest years of the Claudian invasion (c. AD 43–4). What we do not know, for certain, is how long the bridge remained in use. It is fairly safe to assume that it lasted until at least the early years of the fifth century. How much longer it would have survived after the withdrawal of the Roman administration in AD 410, is problematical. But what is pretty certain is that once the bridge finally became unusable it is most unlikely that the surviving Romano-Britons, or Saxons, would have replaced it. It is much more likely that passage across the river then would have been made by way of a ford.

In 1066, when William landed on the south coast, Harold used the old North Road, which runs through Ware, to move his troops from Stamford Bridge to Hastings. We do not have any evidence for a bridge at this time, but for the expedient crossing of several thousand men there must have been at least a reasonable ford there (unless, of course, he diverted through Hertford). To ferry that many men and animals across the river would have been a long, time-consuming task – time that Harold did not have.

By the late twelfth century, if not before, Ware once again could boast a bridge. The Pipe Rolls of Richard I (m.12s. 1191) mentions the bridge as 'having been broken down by the men of Hertford' who were trying to force all traffic to make the passage of the Lea at Hertford, instead of taking the more direct route through Ware. In 1211–14 we know that Sayer de Quincey, Justiciar of England and Lord of the Manor at Ware, chose the moment when Hertford Castle was being besieged by the Dauphin of France, to cast down the iron bars and chains which had been erected by the Bailiff of Hertford to block the passage of wheeled traffic over the bridge and ford. Furthermore, Sayer de Quincey sent a message to the Bailiff of Hertford saying that he would follow the bars and chains into the river if he tried to make anything of it – the Bailiff declined the challenge.

In the later thirteenth century the Hundred Rolls state: 'the bridge [at Ware] is part of the King's Highway'. It is further noted 'the men and Bailiff of Ware have turned aside the road that used to pass by Hertford to Ware, to the detriment of the Town of Hertford'.

There is a cryptic mention of a bridge in 1338–40 (*Cal. Pat. Rolls 1338–40*

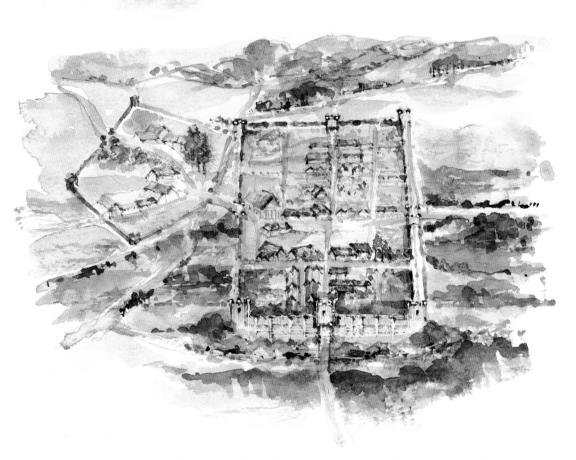

COLOUR PLATE VII. Edward's twin *burghs* at Hertford, looking east. The positions of the *burghs* are approximate and the *burghal* circuits conjectural.

p. 14) in a passage about 'Le Freire Crosse [the brother's cross – presumably an outpreaching station of the Friars Minor] . . . the tenants within the town were bound to make a bridge here . . .' The site of this cross and bridge are unknown.

Accepting that the Roman bridge was just to the east of the present navigation lock, where was the next one? It is possible that by the time we hear again of a bridge at Ware, in 1191, it had moved further downriver in response to the eastward drift of the early Medieval town. When first a bridge was built on the site of the present bridge, at Bridgefoot, is uncertain, but we do know that there was almost certainly a bridge there in Elizabethan times. There is a reference to 'an arched stone bridge at the time of Elizabeth'. It seems pretty certain that this stone bridge was somewhere close to the site of the present bridge because, firstly, the configuration of the valley bottom is at its narrowest here and stone arched bridges were normally only used for spanning fairly narrow crossings. Secondly, there is some confirmation of this in *The Gentlemans Magazine* for 1788. In an article it mentions a bridge of timber, but also talks about 'large pieces of stone from the 'old bridge' . . .' being built into the walls and corners of buildings about the bridge. In the nineteenth century Robert Stephenson's Iron Bridge replaced the eighteenth-century timber bridge.

The reference to an arched stone bridge is interesting and probably unique in the history of bridges at Ware. In Roman and Medieval times the bridges would have been constructed by using large timbers as framework and thick sawn planks as flooring. Of course, timber, even seasoned oak, is susceptible to rot, especially where only partly submerged in water. This means regular maintenance and replacement of damaged members to keep the structure in good working order. A stone bridge has the great advantage of being largely impervious to water. But it is also much more expensive, both in raw materials and in the building. The construction of a stone bridge in Elizabethan times testifies to the wealth of the town, or at the very least a rich patron in Tudor times.

The return to a timber bridge in the eighteenth century may also say something about the wealth, or the attitude, of the Ware people at that time. According to *The Gentlemans Magazine* there were many complaints about the quality of that particular timber bridge. It states 'the flooring of the bridge is unsafe though it has been built barely 25 years'. Apparently there were instances of carts breaking through the bridge planking and falling into the river. From these references in 1788, we may suppose that the stone bridge stood for almost 200 years.

We have talked about the references in various documents to fords at Ware – possibly these were mainly operational in the later Saxon period and again in Norman times. At times these fords must have been quite important crossings of the Lea. We have, for instance, the reference to the bailiff and men of Hertford chaining up the approach to the bridge and ford and also, another time, cutting a deep channel through the middle of the ford, to make it impassable by wheeled traffic.

Earlier we discussed the importance of the Hart ford and, undoubtedly, this would seem to be the most natural position for an all season ford across the Lea in our area. Although it is plain that fords did exist at Ware, they may well have been seasonal in use, perhaps being used quite extensively in summer when the water levels were low, but very little, or not at all during the winter flood conditions.

Medieval Growth and Commerce

The story of Medieval Ware, fascinating as it may be, is largely outside the scope of our intent to tell the story from birth to middle age. There are a number of worthy publications dealing with the later Medieval and post-Medieval history of Ware (see booklist at end of the book). Suffice it to say the change of direction that saw the whole aspect of the town moving eastwards was a turning point in the town's history (no pun intended!). This allowed exploitation of the upper gravel terrace on the north side of the river. This terrace, a reasonably level and slightly elevated platform of land, runs parallel with, but set back far enough from the river margins to be reasonably safe from the danger of flooding. With the easterly change of direction, probably in the late eleventh or early twelfth century, the seeds for the growth of present-day Ware were sown. All that remained to complete the picture was the infilling process, which over the next 300 years saw Ware rise from a small, somewhat scattered village to a bustling market town with a thriving economy, which at its height was second to none in the county.

The story of the dynamic expansion of the malting industry and barge trade, with all the extra traffic to, from and through the town, the proliferation of inns, lodging houses and alehouses, to accommodate the boisterous carters, bargees and travellers, the larger than life characters that were the landlords and landladies of some of the more notorious hostelries, are still to come as we bring our narrative to a close. This is where we must leave Ware still, as it was in the beginning, an important riverside settlement and a major stepping stone for transit between London and the north-east.

POSTSCRIPT

We end our story of the two towns around AD 1300 with both prospering in their own way and Ware now starting to come into its own once again as a major trading centre and staging point on the Great North Road. Its bustling and crowded High Street probably resplendent with market stalls and semi-permanent booths which became formalized over the next 500 years, into the pattern we see today. Brick buildings now occupy the area of the old open market site (the present Market Hall complex) and the old Medieval back rows – represented by East Street and West Street, – were almost certainly established by 1300. Excavations in 1980 at No. 3 West Street revealed remains of a substantial timber-framed building fronting the early back street line and dating to the mid-late 1200s.

The Great Bed of Ware, the spectacular brawls of bargemen and carters, the foundation of a house of the Friars Minor which left the legacy of a fine historic building to the citizens of Ware, are still to come as we take our leave.

Hertford, the County town, had its Royal Castle, both residence of renown and prison of historical significance. Both these things contributed to the prosperity and fame of the town, until at least the time of Elizabeth I. The town may also have hosted Parliament during outbreaks of the plague in London during the sixteenth century. All of this contributed to the town's trade and revenue. Unfortunately, Hertford suffered particularly severely from the effects of the plague in the late sixteenth century, a setback which was to take many years to rectify.

Appendix A

THE HERTFORD BURGHS: A SURVEY OF THE EVIDENCE
Sal Garfi

This appendix has been extracted from a survey carried out by Sal Garfi during his time with The Hart Archaeological Unit as Field Officer, in the early 1970s. It is considered to have much of interest for the serious student of town development and general reader alike and suggests a realistic view of the importance of Hertford and its relation to London. Our thanks are extended to Sal Garfi for the opportunity to present some of his ideas and conclusions from his work in Hertford.

INTRODUCTION

The first written reference to a place called Hertford are those relating to the Synod of AD 673, which states that the religious meeting was held at *Herutford*. That this is our town seems doubtful however, though local sentiment still appears quite persistent in attributing this event as taking place in Hertford, Hertfordshire. The most definite references to the early borough are the AD 912-13 entries in the Anglo-Saxon Chronicle stating that the two *burghs* of Hertford (Heortford) were constructed so as to protect Edward the Elder's northern flank in the early stages of his campaign against the Danes. After this, coin evidence tells us that a community continued on the site, up to and beyond the time of Domesday Book. In the early Medieval period an important castle was positioned close to the ford. But throughout the Middle Ages the borough gradually declined in riches and importance.

The object of this survey is to review the history and archaeology of Hertford. It is hoped that, at least for the Anglo-Saxon period, Hertford may be put into its proper perspective. The borough's position and the political climate in which it was founded, as well as its Medieval history, all point to the town's foundation as that of a fort, rather than that of a (fortified) market town. The growth of the Medieval town, in 'plan units'(Fig. 13, p. 80) is charted and discussed and the town's relationship to London is reviewed, especially in the Saxon and early Medieval periods.

HERTFORD AND LONDON

In all, the position of Hertford is such that the borough is well situated on the River Lea, at a point where it can serve as a hub for a network of waterways radiating from around the ford. These water routes accommodating river traffic can link – along with the possible east–west Ware–Verulamium road and the Ermine Street – the south with the hinterland of Hertfordshire. Hertford is a bottleneck collecting and funnelling southbound traffic while directing and spreading northbound traffic; servicing London, via the Ermine Street and the River Lea. This is very important, for it at least puts Hertford into a good strategic position concerning London.

London's territory, which probably included a good deal of Hertfordshire, quite probably had the River Lea as a northern limit, putting Hertford into a frontier situation. Throughout the Anglo-Saxon period London itself was very much on a frontier; that is especially manifest in the City's south-westerly position in its own

Diocese. London sat in the corner of a great district including Essex, east Hertfordshire and Middlesex. This, the City's Medieval See, which is almost certainly older
than the shire boundaries as we know them, would have thrust Hertford into a key
position.

Hertford is also north of the Reading beds and the London clays, those very
heavy claylands which surrounded London and support a superb natural barrier
of heavy oak woodland, making up what can be considered a great deal of the
City's immediate northern territory. Hertford is thus sandwiched between the south-
east end of the Chilterns, which probably made up the north-western extent of
London's lands, and the South Hertfordshire Plateau which extends from Ware, to
Radlett and southwards into Greater London.

This upland area north of London rises to nearly 110 metres OD near Epping
Green, the high ground west of the Lea Valley and Ermine Street and east of Watling
Street. These physical barriers, which Hertford appears to be integral with, probably
allowed the City of London to be quite isolated from the series of events associated
with the coming of the Anglo-Saxons. And this no doubt contributed to the City
having a special status, at least during the late Anglo-Saxon period, which was
reaffirmed by the twelfth-century charters granting special rights to the citizens of
London.

Though probably quite early, the Oxford, Chiltern and Pinner Grim's Ditches
could have served to mark out the limits of territory under the sway of London. It
appears that the ditches could have been constructed by Saxon newcomers and
their purpose appears to be essentially valley-enclosing, along the fringes of the
natural barriers mentioned above. From northern Middlesex to the western end of
the Chilterns we are confronted by a series of boundary ditches facing towards
London and built by a population approaching from the north or north-west. This
population consisted mainly of farmers who were exploiting the valleys and partially clearing the forested claylands in or about them. And they did not go into
the lands of London.

EARLY HISTORY

Bede, in his *Ecclesiastical History*, recounts the decisions of the council called by
Theodore of Tarsus, Archbishop of Canterbury, at the Synod on 24 September AD
673. It is widely presumed that the place of the Synod was Hertford, Hertfordshire.
However, there is no real reason why this has to be so. There appears a good
possibility that the Synod was held at Hartford, Huntingdonshire. Firstly, at the
time of the Synod, Hertford was in the diocese of London and Wine who had
recently bought the bishopric of London from Wulfhere, King of Mercia, was not
even present at the meeting nor were his proxies. Secondly, according to canon
(chapter) eight of the decisions taken at the Synod, it was stated: 'That no bishop
claim precedence over another out of ambition: seniority of consecration shall alone
determine precedence.' Now Bisi, the East Anglian bishop, is mentioned together
with Archbishop Theodore, separately from the other attending bishops and his
consecration is believed to have been later than some of the other attendant bishops.
Perhaps this was so because Bisi was the host bishop and his See located at Hartford,
Huntingdonshire. No material of the seventh century has yet to come to light to
support the idea of a settlement at Hertford, Herts. It might be conjectured that
Hertford's only *raison d'être* probably came about during the Danish wars.

The Anglo-Saxon Chronicle tells us about the power struggle between the Danes and the Saxons led by Alfred. The entry for AD 895 describes how the Danes came up the Lea and Alfred opposed them . . . the final outcome saw the Danes repulsed and fleeing across country to Bridgenorth on Severn leaving their ships somewhere along the Lea (see Appendix D).

Derek Renn wrote:

> The only large enclosure, big enough to act as a fort and harbour for the ships, beside the Lea about 20 miles above London that I know, is the outer bailey of Hertford Castle. This 'bailey' is rather anomalous in that, instead of simply being attached to the inner bailey ditch at two points, its bank continues round two sides of the inner bailey as a narrow causeway between two ditches. Further, the outer 'bailey' is much smaller in usable area than the inner bailey. The explanation could be that the outer enclosure is the older, and the inner bailey was created to enclose a more defensible area for a smaller body of men than those originally intended to occupy the area (D. Renn: *Medieval Castles in Hertfordshire*, 1971).

Derek Renn's hypothesis is very tantalizing but unproven as up to the present no controlled excavations have been undertaken in the Castle grounds. However, if Renn's suggestion is proven correct, then the AD 895 Chronicle reference would definitely relate to Hertford. Nonetheless, the reference to the positioning of Alfred's forces so as to protect the English from the Danes at harvest time does suggest an early settlement, perhaps at Hertford.

The events along the Lea in AD 895 took place during a phase of consolidation on the part of Alfred. During his early reign, from AD 871 to 878 the Danes held much of the initiative and it was in the balance whether or not the whole of England would fall into their grasp. During the middle years of his reign, AD 878 to 891, Alfred was involved in securing and demarcating his frontiers. The events that took place along the Lea, the Danelaw boundary during this period, could have been trying to nibble away at extra land along the frontier. During the latter period of AD 891 to 899, the last foreign threat came, culminating with the break-up of the Danish 'great horde' in AD 896, leaving Alfred's last three years peaceful ones.

THE FOUNDATION OF THE BURGHS

However, the most important reference, directly related to Hertford, is also in the Anglo-Saxon Chronicle and refers to events of AD 912–13, during the reign of Edward the Elder. It states that in AD 911 Aethelred the ealdorman of Mercia and brother-in-law of Edward the Elder died and King Edward took over London and Oxford and all the lands which belonged thereto. Before the end of 912 King Edward had the more northerly fortress at Hertford built, between the Maran (Mimram) and the Beane and the Lea. Then afterwards, the summer in AD 913, between Rogation Sunday and midsummer, King Edward went with part of his forces to Maldon in Essex, and encamped there whilst the earthwork at Witham was being built and stockaded: and a good number of people who had earlier been under Danish domination submitted to him. Another part of his forces meanwhile built the fortress at Hertford on the southern bank of the Lea. By doing this Edward kept a check on his north flank against the Danes of Cambridge and Bedford. Throughout all this period the site of Hertford was on the Danelaw boundary which ran from Chester, along Watling Street to the Lea, then down to London and along the Thames to the sea. The Lea, being integral with the Danelaw frontier, meant that Hertford was in a frontier location, especially in relation to the lands of London and Oxford. As a good tactical move Edward fortified the ford because, as the geographic position of Hertford illustrates it is in the middle of a vast frontier of natural defences surrounding London. It is a main focal point for transportation and communication routes; thus a centre of control and observation (at least in a military sense). By controlling the Lea at Hertford Edward kept London, an important base, secure.

Edward, Alfred's son, came to the throne in AD 899, and from that year until AD 902, the new king was threatened by his cousin Aethelwold, son of Aethelred. However, after Edward showed a force of arms against the upstart cousin, Aethelwold ran to the Danes of Northumbria where he was received wholeheartedly. In AD 901 he came to the surface in Essex with a foreign fleet and in AD 902 he, with an East Anglian army, raided Mercia and northern Wessex. There was a wry twist of fate as a sequel to this. After Edward invaded East Anglia in retaliation for Aethelwold's incursion and defeated the enemy army, the Kentishmen under Edward disobeyed an order to withdraw and were caught up by the Danes. The battle that ensued, with the Danes keeping the place of slaughter, however saw the death of Aethelwold, the Danish king and another Englishman of the highest rank. In AD 909 hostilities were resumed with Edward taking the initiative. An English army of West Saxons and Mercians invaded Danish Northumbria for five weeks and forced them to accept conditions of peace imposed by Edward. This invasion was countered in AD 910 by an advance into Mercia by the Northumbrian Danes, culminating in the battle of Tettenhall, Staffordshire. In this battle the power of Northumbria was crippled thus paving the way for a West Saxon advance into East Anglia.

In AD 911, after the death of the ealdorman Aethelred of Mercia, Edward the Elder advanced eastwards; the reconquest of Danish England was commenced. Edward's first move was to secure the lands of Oxford and London, guarding his northern flank by building the North *burgh* of Hertford. It is in this milieu of burgh construction and settlement, on the part of Edward and his sister Aethelflead, the wife of the ealdorman Aethelred, that we ought to view the position of Hertford in the early tenth century. Throughout the English campaigns of this period it appears that the creation, and/or refortification of defensive positions (*burghs*), were actions taken by Edward and his sister, as military expedients. In the first place Edward built Hertford to secure one of his flanks. Such an establishment need not have included the provision of a civil centre.

Now after some campaigning in the west Edward resumed his eastern advance, marching north to Buckingham and building a set of dual fortresses on either side of the Ouse. This is quite reminiscent of Hertford and the move resulted in the submission of the Bedfordshire Danes. In AD 915, after a season of campaigning, he eventually took Bedford itself, and he refortified the town with a new fortress south of the Ouse. In AD 916 Edward decided to reassert his pressure in Essex. He now secured his fortress in Witham from a seaborne raid by constructing a fort at Maldon. At the same time, his sister was fortifying Mercia.

In all, the English *burghs* of the first quarter of the tenth century appear to be the result of, if not integral with, the campaigns of the Wessex–Mercian power in reclaiming the Danelaw. In this the *burghs* constructed by Edward and his sister seem different from those of the 'Burghal Hidage', a system whose outline, probably, was laid down by Alfred in the years immediately preceding the Danish invasion of AD 892. That is, during the middle part of his reign, during his years of consolidation, when the future defences of Wessex were being considered and strengthened. Alfred wanted to secure and defend his lands in case of future hostilities and to supply redoubts for the local populace. By the early part of the tenth century no village in Sussex, Surrey and Wessex east of the Tamar was distant more than twenty miles from a fortress which formed a unit in a planned scheme of national defence. In Wessex, Alfred wanted places of refuge, supply, administration and, probably in the long run, markets. Later, during the wars of Edward and Aethelflead, tactical decisions had to be made concerning the acquisition and control of new territory. A plan had to be in existence for the supply and maintenance of forces in the field, along with considerations given towards the protection of these forces in case the tides of war turned against the English levies. Alfred wanted to protect his kingdom; his son and daughter, while on the offensive, wanted to check the enemy in the field and secure territory taken by force or by treaty.

MINTS

Stenton remarks: 'Edward, on the verge of old age, was responsible for the good order of a composite state twice as large as the kingdom which he inherited from his father.' He reorganized most of the Danelaw, and after his sister's death gained control of Mercia. Both he and his sister planted and fortified towns. The England welded together by Edward the Elder passed on to his son Aethelstan on 4 September AD 925; Edward had died in July AD 924. It is during the reign of Aethelstan that we find the first overt English statements of law referring to mints:

> 'We declare . . . that there shall be one coinage throughout the King's domain and that there shall be no minting except in a port. And if a minter be convicted of striking bad money, the hand with which he was guilty shall be cut off and set up on the mint smithy . . . In Canterbury there shall be seven minters; four of them the King's; two, the archbishop's; one, the abbots. In Rochester, three; two of them the King's; and one, the bishop's. In London there shall be eight; in Winchester, six; in Lewes, two; in Wareham, two; in Dorchester on Thames, one; in Exeter, two; in Shaftsbury, two; in each other *burgh*, one . . .'

Hertford was one of those 'other *burghs*' in Aethelstan's law. In fact, coins were struck at Hertford almost continually up until, and after, the Norman conquest save during the reigns of Edmund (AD 939–46), Eadred (AD 946–55), Harthacnut (AD 1040–2) and Harold II (Jan–Oct AD 1066).

The existence of a mint at Hertford, does pose certain archaeological problems, however, especially concerning the 'nature' of the Saxon settlement. As a *burgh* of Edward the Elder, Hertford's function may have been extremely specialized, i.e. as a point for military control; with, during its foundation by Edward, no plans on the part of the king desiring the growth of Hertford as a centre for the surrounding countryside. Hertford, as a probable military centre, outlived its vocation with the end of Edward's Danish wars. The ascendancy of Ware in the twelfth century only exaggerated this by becoming, in effect, a more important town. But the existence of a mint at Hertford could cause the borough to be viewed as a major amenities centre, like other new English towns before and after the Norman conquest. For instance, of the three surviving charters of Alfred relating to urban places, all deal with trading rights, or refer to aspects of trade. Therefore, others have presumed that Hertford was an urban centre in the late Saxon period and this is considered so, because Hertford's foundation is that of a *burgh*. But how far can this be taken? Certainly, a mint existed at Hertford, but was the town anything more than a fortress (during the Danish wars) instead of a fortified town (during the Danish wars and after)? Local historians by virtue of their vocation appear to have viewed Hertford in an exalted way. Probably, this ought to be revised. Stenton remarked:

> In the reigns of Aethelred II and Cnut, when the evidence has become copious, there is no doubt that moneyers were established, not only in the large commercial centres of the east, the county towns of the Midlands, and most of the *burghs* mentioned in the Burghal Hideage, but also in places where the trading community must have been a mere appendage to a royal manor. There cannot have been any large concentration of burgesses and there can hardly have been more than the most rudimentary of fortifications at Aylesbury or Crewkerne or Bruton. Cadbury in Somerset, where coins were struck for both Aethelred and Cnut, and Horndon in Essex, where they were struck for Edward the Confessor, were not even royal manors in 1066 and Domesday Book gives no hint of anything unusual in their past. Each of them had probably been short-lived *burghs*, like the *novum oppidum* called *Beorchore*, which Aethelred II visited in AD 1007, but of which there is no other record. Even so, Cadbury certainly and Horndon probably, cannot have been important places, and their coins increase the probability that in the first half of the eleventh century every *burgh*, whatever its size, had been a centre for the issue of currency (Sir Frank Stenton: *Anglo-Saxon England*, 1971).

Though Hertford is a county town in the eleventh century, the latter part of Stenton's remarks above, appears most applicable. It is interesting to note that the idea of Hertford outliving its military usefulness, after the Danish Wars, is consistent with the fates of other *burghs* of the tenth and eleventh centuries. It has been observed that boroughs, originally of Roman foundation, refounded or repaired during the Danish wars and belonging to either the Danes or the English, had the greatest chance of survival as settlements into the twelfth century; three quarters continued to hold some kind of rank. Those *burghs*, based on Roman foundations, lasted because their positions (e.g. on Roman roads) were well chosen and useful for trade and military purposes. But those newly founded, were established to deal with a unique war-time situation, therefore, the chances of survival when the military need was taken away became less. The Roman towns were amenities centres serving given geographic and political areas with planned and natural access routes (roads and rivers). The new English towns were sited strategically, to subdue enemy armies and consolidate conquered territory. Of these, only just over one third survived into the Medieval period. This specialization probably contributed to Hertford's eventual insignificance in the Middle Ages.

POST AD 1066 AND DECLINE

According to the Domesday Book Hertford had, during Edward the Confessor's time, 146 burgesses. Turnor felt that because of this, Hertford was a town of considerable note during the early Middle Ages. He pointed out, that towns presumably larger than Hertford, had scarcely double the burgesses. He cites Exeter as having only 315 houses; Canterbury 262; Warwick 225; Northampton 60; and Norwich 738. Nonetheless, Hertford still answered for only ten hides before 1066, with the allusion that it did not do so in 1086. In relation to the rest of the country, it could appear that Hertford was quite prosperous before the Norman Conquest. Saxon Hertford may have been in reality the most important market in the Shire. Comparing its number of burgesses with information about other communities at the time of Domesday, one could see that Hertford could not be matched. Ware, its eventual rival, had only 125 householders; St Albans had only 46 burgesses; and Cheshunt could only account for ten merchants.

The twelfth century saw the start of a period of consistent decline for the borough of Hertford (Fig. 15). Previously Hertford had a monopoly of traffic in the area, which was threatened by the existence of a bridge and possibly ford at Ware. This bridge the men of Hertford destroyed in 1191. Hertford claimed the tolls collected from the Ware bridge and ford as its rightful revenue. But during the wars of 1215-16 when most of the county and the area around Hertford must have been affected in a detrimental way, the men of Ware disregarded Hertford's toll rights. It appears that Hertford did not regain its title to the Ware bridge until after 1247. Hertford claimed the revenues, and therefore controlled the passages through Thele and Hatfield, and stipulated that no markets were to be held within a seven-mile radius around Hertford, on the borough's two market days of Thursday and Saturday. Until the reign of Edward III, Hertford's market held on Thursday was held on a Wednesday.

1258 saw another attack on the bridge and ford at Ware by the men of Hertford. Notable in this dispute was the digging of a ditch across the London-Ware road so as to add an extra deterrent to traffic wishing to cross the River Lea at Ware. But, by 1274, the overland passage through Ware seemed to have become firmly established, leaving Hertford out of the mainstream of north–south traffic. A fate which the borough would, most assuredly, have suffered at an earlier date, if the Hertford burgesses were not so vehement in their attempts at keeping a monopoly over the traffic crossing the Lea in East Hertfordshire. Hertford was not saved by its being a nodal point of four rivers and their traffic. Those valley routes never became major ones and unfortunately, the routes that have become important in east Hertfordshire mainly bypass the borough.

For a while river traffic was prevented from travelling freely to Hertford. This was due to the bailiffs of Ware controlling the weirs on the Lea at Ware. Tolls were not handed over to Hertford in 1277, though it appears that the men of Ware eventually renewed the custom. In all, the value of the tolls collected at Ware were on the increase during this period, reflecting the greater use of Ware as a crossing point of the Lea. Hertford had lost to Ware the passage of the Lea and the possession of the main road and this constituted the best asset of the borough.

The borough's position in AD 911–12, along with the other *burghs* founded by Edward the Elder, testifies to river travel as the most effective means of transport before the Norman conquest. Probably it was river travel which fostered the foundation of communities along the Lea valley, south-east of Hertford, during the post-Roman period, which in turn caused the present valley (London) road to follow a course, north of Tottenham mainly to the east of Ermine Street, so as to link the Lea valley settlements. Presumably, this occurred during the Middle Ages when an increase in road usage and haulage took place, thus assisting greatly in the ascent of Ware.

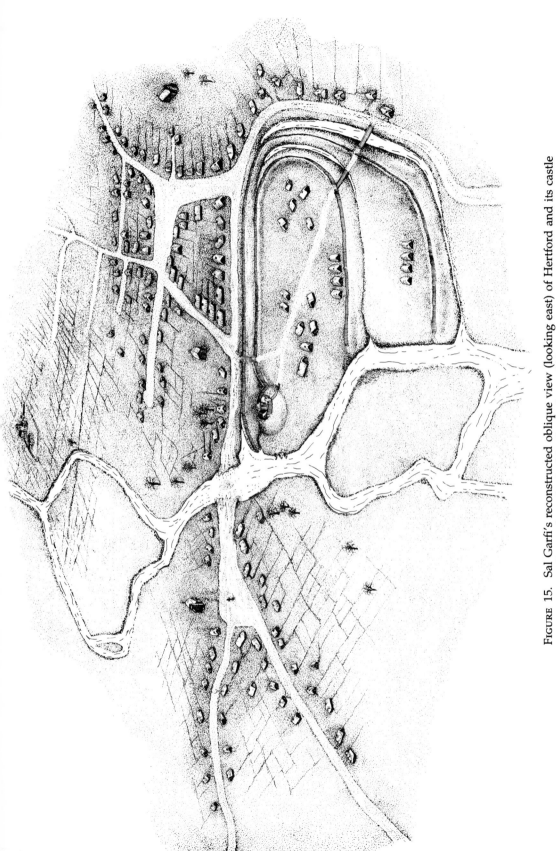

FIGURE 15. Sal Garfi's reconstructed oblique view (looking east) of Hertford and its castle as it may have looked in the early twelfth century.

Since Hertford was the centre of a waterways system penetrating into the hinter-land of eastern Hertfordshire, just a glance at the map would show how Hertford's trade and importance could have been impaired if road traffic began taking pre-cedence over river traffic. For instance, goods travelling northwards along Ermine Street and its diversion towards the Lea valley settlements, would not need to travel the detour to Hertford if a bridge was open at Ware. In fact, such a valley route would cause the site of Ware to gain in importance and as a result the Ermine Street north of Tottenham may have become largely redundant, along with the diversion from Hertford Heath to Hertford which connected the borough with Ermine Street. Also, north of Tottenham, Ermine Street has only been preserved in short stretches as lanes and field boundaries. This is especially the case around Hertford Heath.

Indications of an increase in road usage in the Medieval period do exist. For example the Gough Map, dating to the middle of the fourteenth century, shows what are considered to be well established 'carting routes' radiating from London. Also in 1333, a great number of writs were drawn up ordering religious heads to send carts and wagons with horses northwards, so as to carry tents and other provisions for the king's Scottish Campaign.

It is unfortunate that Hertford's assets, other than those related to revenues collected by a monopoly on through traffic, do not appear to have been very great. The wool and cloth trade does not seem to have been much developed; there was no merchants' guild in the borough. The agricultural wealth of the borough seems not to have been very great. The Pope Nicholas taxation statistics of 1291, show the following valuations:

Hertford	c. 1d per acre
St Albans	c. 3d per acre
Sawbridgworth	c. 5d per acre
Ware	c. 7d per acre
Berkhamsted	c. 4d per acre
Hitchin	c. 2½d per acre

The statistics speak for themselves. The borough's taxable value was by now on the decline. In 1290 it is stated that St Albans had more and richer taxpayers and even Cheshunt was larger than Hertford. In 1308 the taxable value of Hertford, in relation to Cheshunt and Ware was:

Hertford	£ 7 16s 8d
Cheshunt	£12 11s 4d
Ware	£14 55s 5¼d

Hertford was taxed at only one half the worth of Ware; a very bad state of affairs for the shire borough.

The decline of Hertford throughout the Middle Ages caused the writers of the Victoria County History to remark that, 'during the fourteenth and fifteenth cen-turies Hertford must have been no more than a village'. Also contributing to the general decline was the Black Death. In 1428 there were not ten householders in the Parish of St Nicholas or that of St Mary-the-Less.

In all, the predicament of Hertford throughout the Medieval period causes one to wonder what truly was the worth of the borough? Militarily, the town was initially important. But save for this and the borough's administrative function why did Hertford 'hang on'? Perhaps Turnor, in a footnote, puts it best:

The importance which is attached by many writers to the town of Hertford, during the middle ages, arises doubtless from its connection with the castle, on which it was in some measure dependent . . . Its governors were invariably men of high rank and noble birth, either partaking the confidence of their sovreign, or, on the contrary, of such power and stability, as to be regardless of his favour. From the character of these high-minded nobles there can be but little question that the castle partook largely of the hospitality and munificence, attended with that martial splendour and those busy scenes, which the residences of the Barons in those days almost always displayed: and such being the fact, that the advantages accruing to the town and its inhabitants from the circumstance, stamped it with a consequence, which otherwise it could hardly have received . . .'(Turnor: *History of Hertford*).

THE STREET LAYOUT

The twin *burghs* which Edward the Elder founded at Hertford is something we only know of through the references in the Anglo-Saxon Chronicle. The certainty of Hertford's plan and location, as of AD 912–13, is something which is definitely not known.

To deal with this problem it is essential to look at the townscape in great detail; more specifically, from a cartographic point of view. This is more especially so when the town plan is the one and only major artefact we have to deal with. It should be pointed out that this artefact is not merely an ancient street plan, but covers the rest of the built-up area as well. It consists of three distinct complexes of plan elements: The streets and their mutual association in a street system; the individual land parcels or plots and their aggregation in street blocks with distinct patterns; finally the buildings, or more precisely their block-plans and the arrangement of these in the town plan as a whole.

Precise documentation concerning the town's extent and development comes very late, the first being Norden's Survey of 1621 (John Norden: *A Description of Hertfordshire*). This though only represents the town's revival during the sixteenth century. Archaeological evidence is variable, mainly due to the fact that comparatively little work has been undertaken in the borough centre. For the Saxon period, we have a scatter of findspots, largely Saxo-Norman in date. But of course these represent, not a pattern, but only the places where there has been an opportunity for collection of material. All in all, the only way in which a model of Hertford's development can be created is through the town's street plan. To do so, it would be useful to employ the approach which enlists a method of 'plan analysis'. That is, an attempt at the recognition of distinct plan units, which are illustrations and/or manifestations, representing the growth and/or pattern of a town's development and layout. Such recognition depends on the careful scrutiny of plan detail such as the behaviour of street spaces and their bounding street lines, the shape, size, orientation and grouping of plots. All such evidence leading to the identification of the 'seams' along which the genetically significant plan units are knit together.

To appreciate the 'seams' and plan units of a town, one needs to be able to appreciate the contours of the town's site. This can be most telling and illustrative and is especially so in the case of Hertford. Since no contour map of the borough exists, Fig. 13 was assembled by interpolating levels from OS map spot heights, random spot heights, archaeological information and other field observations. It shows up quite clearly the two high and dry settlement points, which constitute the topography of central Hertford. One is a knoll, while the other is a terrace or shelf; these serving as steps across the River Lea's flood plain. From the knoll, at Old Cross, there is a very good view up and down the course of the Lea. This knoll is at a higher OD level than that part of Hertford south of the Lea on the terrace or shelf. And, moreover, it is situated amidst the Rivers Mimram, Beane and Lea (as the Anglo-Saxon Chronicle so describes the position of Hertford's North *burgh*). So Old Cross fulfills the requirements of a foundation located for strategic reasons along an inland waterway.

In this survey attempts at trying to discern plan units will be limited to analysing the borough, as its extent was illustrated in John Speed's map of *c*. 1610. The modern cartographic records for Hertford are not bad, therefore, plan analysis would be most useful to try to illustrate the periods prior to the publication of John Speed's map. The most useful plans to work with, for Hertford, are the Ordnance Survey 25" and 50" maps; both modern editions and those of the later Victorian period. Since Hertford straddles the River Lea and history tells us that the town was a dual *burgh*, the borough's plan analysis should adopt a dual approach. Firstly, Old Cross, quite likely Edward's North *burgh*, will be dealt with. Secondly, the part of Hertford south of the Lea will be looked at and described, for the sake of discussion, as the South *burgh*. But, as has already been pointed out, we cannot be certain whether or not the street plan and position of Hertford north, and especially south of the Lea, represents Edward's two *burghs* and so this should always be borne in mind.

Any conclusions from a plan analysis of Hertford will only be a model for the Saxon and Medieval towns. Hopefully it will provide material for discussion and perhaps guidance for archaeological explorations.

THE NORTH BURGH

The area around Old Cross, the North *burgh*, is very village-like in plan (see Fig. 13). It appears to consist of a minimum of five plan units. They are: (1) Old Cross itself, a small square or open central place, into which burgage plots would face and out of which roads radiate; (2) St Andrew Street, leaving Old Cross in a west-south-westerly direction, as far as St Andrews Church; (3) Cowbridge, leaving Old Cross in a west-north-westerly direction as far as the River Beane; (4) the western-most extent of St Andrew Street, including St Andrews Church. And finally (5) market or open space colonization in Old Cross.

The relationships of these plan units suggests that the Old Cross plan unit is probably the oldest. Traffic from south of the Lea would have gone directly into the open space, via the ford and/or bridge. It would have left via either St Andrew Street or Cowbridge. The church of St Mary-the-Less was situated on the east side of Old Cross. At the time of Speed a market cross was shown as still in position; which gives this plan unit its name. The tenements along the south-east side of Old Cross, in the sloping ground from the middle of the market place down to the Lea, are probably the result of market colonization. These may date especially to the time after the ford probably went out of use. This would leave Mill Bridge as the only means of crossing the Lea. This could account for the market place of Old Cross being partly on level ground and partly on ground sloping down towards the Lea.

Both Cowbridge and St Andrew Street represent ribbon development. St Andrew Street, however, has grown up in at least two phases. The first phase of growth

unit (2), represents roadside development spreading as far westward as, approximately, the 40 metre contour. At this point there is a kink and narrowing in the
road at Brewhouse Lane, representing a 'seam' between two plan units. At this
narrowing of the road we find St Andrews Church, which was probably constructed
outside the area of greatest tenement concentration, which was most likely in the
thirteenth century. Later tenements started accumulating along St Andrew Street,
infringing into the street west of Brewhouse Lane, becoming plan unit (4).

THE SOUTH BURGH

When looking at Hertford south of the River Lea, one can locate up to eleven plan
units (see Fig. 13). Some may be considered components or subdivisions of other
units. For the sake of clarity it is probably best to point out as many of the 'seams'
or 'fixation lines' as are discernible, thus delineating quite a large number of plan
units for the small area of Hertford's South *burgh*. 'Fixation lines', like 'seams',
represent phases in a town's growth; towns do not grow steadily but rather
unevenly with periods of rapid extension followed by periods of standstill. In
these periods of stability the margin of growth is demarcated by a distinctive line,
sometimes a physical feature such as a town wall, or a sharp break of slope. At
other times a non-physical feature such as a property boundary remains to point
out the extent of a developmental phase; the 'seam' between two or more plan
units.

In the case of Hertford's South *burgh* it is very hard to place the plan units in
any historic order or sequence. The area of the town's earliest phases, i.e. the Saxon,
we may never be able to pin down without adequate excavation. Therefore, of the
plan units here described, no defined sequence will be attempted; Hertford's plan
south of the river appears composite in nature. It exhibits what is probably a
planned area north of Fore Street; but whether or not Fore Street, as a high street,
was in existence before or after the planned area to its north, is something which
we cannot say at present.

The eleven plan units, in this part of Hertford, are as follows: (1) a central unit
consisting of the four blocks created by the junction of Bull Plain, Maidenhead
Street, the westernmost end of Railway Street (sometimes in the past known as
Back Street) and Market Place – this is the probable planned area north of Fore
Street, mentioned above; (2) the Castle (including the area of the courses of its
former ditches which are now built over); (3) the south-east side of Parliament
Square, taking in Bell Lane and extending as far as Church Street; (4), (5) and (6)
are the tenements along Fore Street; (7) the tenements on the south side of Castle
Street; (8) the area of Bircherley Green; (9) market colonization; (10) West Street;
(11) the remaining plan components.

Plan units (1), (2), (3), (4) and (5) most probably represent the Medieval southern
borough of Hertford. They illustrate the composite nature of the plan, showing that
the borough probably developed in stages. The tenements of unit (1) are small and
compact, quite different from the tenements in unit (3) and especially along Fore
Street (units (4) (5) and (6)) where they are long and thin, illustrating a kind of
ribbon development. A ditch, partly excavated by Hertford Museum in 1973, behind
31 and 33 Railway Street, is believed to be 'Saxo-Norman' in date. This could
represent an eastern boundary for the early Medieval borough. But the excavator
was not sure that this necessarily was the case. Nonetheless H. C. Andrews (one
time Curator of Hertford Museum) noted that:

the Gulphs, alias Ashbourne Ditch, alias Wall Ditch . . . bringing water down from the uplands of Brickendon today, takes an abrupt turn from north to east by All Saints Churchyard, opposite the east end of the church and then follows a lengthy course to the Lea, some distance from the town. This may have been one branch of the Ashbourne Ditch, but there is clear evidence that the main ditch continued straight on by the west wall of the Grammar School, down the east side of the Dimsdale Arms yard, across Fore Street, down the east side of the Corn Exchange, then across Railway Street and through Bircherley (Butchery) Green to the former Dye's Dipping Place on the River Lea. This, incidentally, is also where in later times the town sewer was discharged. When the Talbot Arms, next to the Dimsdale Arms Hotel, and the Post Office were built in 1891 and again when a building was being added to the small brewery in Railway Street, the foundations had to pierce through a thick substratum of the washed sand of the Ashbourne Ditch . . .

The exact position of Dye's Dipping Place is not known, but it is believed to have been in the north-west corner of the old Hertford Bus Station. Therefore, the ditch excavated in 1973 could very well have been the extension of the Ashbourne Ditch, mentioned above by H. C. Andrews; because of its length and position it could have served as an eastern boundary to the borough in the late Saxon and/or early Medieval periods. The alignments of plan units (4), (5) and (6) appear to support this theory. The tenements of unit (4) are quite parallel with Church Street, but all of a sudden, with unit (5), the tenements change their alignment to become parallel with, what could be, the projected line of the Ashbourne Ditch. Unit (5) on both sides of Fore Street, extends eastwards for a short distance beyond the probable line of the ditch, but it must be noted that conclusions from the 1973 excavation suggest that the ditch was backfilled in the twelfth century. Excavations by The Hart Archaeological Unit, in advance of the Central Area redevelopment, confirmed the line of this ditch and the conclusions reached earlier, that the ditch had been backfilled in the twelfth or early thirteenth century. Also, the 'seam' between units (5) and (6) marks, as well as a change in tenement alignments, a bend in Fore Street. At this point the Ashbourne Ditch, filled in or not, no longer exerted any influence on the tenements. Now, outside the probable town limit, a ribbon-like suburban growth began; this is manifest in plan unit (6). Further linear development can be seen along Castle Street and West Street (units (7) and (10) respectively). Market colonization (9) is evident in Parliament Square and Market Place, with Bircherley Green ((8) and (11)) filling in the rest of the townscape.

Appendix B

THE MINT AT HERTFORD
David R. Fish

These are some records I have found relating to the Hertford mint and its coins and some of the find spots. To record all would take too long for this short study. The actual site of the mint is not known. Suggested spots are the town centre to the south of the Lea, somewhere in the Bengeo area and Old Cross just to the north of the river. Archaeological investigation has been undertaken in most of these areas but as yet the mint remains undetected.

The first mint-signed coins come in the reign of Aethelstan (AD 924–39). The coin is a two-line type, the moneyer is ABONEL, date period AD 925–7. It is a unique penny found in the Forum hoard, now (with the remainder of that hoard) in the Museo Nazionale at Rome. It combines an obverse of the cross types (BMC:I) with the reverse of the cross types (BMC:V). The obverse of the two types are generally similar but may be distinguished by the fact that on the two-line type REX is followed by some abbreviation of TOtius BRIttanniae (or rarely, at one or two Mercian mints, of SAXORUM). The moneyer's name is ABONEL which is followed by the unusual MON TO before the mint name HIORTFD.

Where then is the mint at this time? It is likely that the site was close to water for the process of metal smelting and cooling. Access to a wooded area for charcoal for the firing would not have posed much of a problem, as much of the higher slopes around Bengeo must have supported substantial forestation.

Maldon also shares the same moneyer, ABONEL, and a die-link is known between the two Boroughs.

Three specimens of Aethelstan's Crowned Bust type (BMC:VIII) are known from Hertford, two probably from the same dies. One is in the Forum hoard No. 211 and the other is Copenhagen No. 694. On the third coin is the same obverse but a different reverse die, from the Berlin Cabinet. The moneyer is again ABONEL, followed by the normal MO. The mint on both dies reads HIORT. A small feature found on both die reverses, is a trefoil of pellets in the field at nine o'clock. It is curious that all three specimens should be in Continental collections. Two are from local hoards; the provenance of the third is not known.

ABONEL is an interesting name and its origin must remain uncertain. It is not recorded on coins of Edward the Elder, but in the form ABENEL is found on coins of Aethelstan II of East Anglia. The British Museum Catalogue records the same reading on a coin which it attributes to Alfred (BMC:190) but the obverse reading suggests that this may be of Aethelstan II. The name, in a variety of forms, is found in the St Edmund Memorial coinage (e.g. BMC:117–28). It is not found, however, for an Aethelstan (of all England) on any mint-signed coins other than those of Hertford and Maldon. Because of this it is fairly safe to attribute the unsigned coins of this king to one or other of these mints, although the preference is for Hertford, which may have produced coins at a much earlier date than hitherto found.

Although a full coin of the Circumscription (cross) type has not been recorded, it is not impossible that this type was struck at Hertford. The Diademed Bust type (BMC:VII) is also not recorded for this mint.

Aethelstan enacted new coinage laws at Grately during his reign. The statute gives the quota of moneyer's for each burgh and the name of the moneyer, together with that of the town in which he minted, but does not say where the mint house stood. But from thereon the reverse of all coins has the name of the mint along with the moneyers.

Although no mint-signed coins are known of Hertford during Eadmund's reign, a few coins with the name ABENEL and ABUNEL are known of the two-line type (BMC:I). The lettering on these are of a type which is associated with the southern part of the country and to that of Hertford Mint coins.

Eadwig (AD 955–9). Again ABENAL appears as a moneyer, this time on a mint-signed coin of the three-line type (BMC:II); the mint name is HIR. There is, however, an extra cross in the obverse field which may be compared with the trefoil of pellets in the reverse field of Aethelstan's Crowned Bust type. Brooke, when recording this coin in his report on 'British Museum Acquisitions since the Catalogue was published', described it as 'Hertford?' (NC 1925, p. 364), but was, by the time he published his *English Coins*, prepared to drop the question mark. This must surely be justified; the combination of the mint reading HIR with the moneyer's name ABENEL can hardly point to any other mint than Hertford. This is the only type recorded for Eadwig under this mint.

During Eadgar's reign (AD 959–75) an early portrait (Crowned Bust type BMC:V) is a unique coin of Hertford, the moneyer is again ABENEL. The mint name reads HIRT. ABENEL is not recorded again during this reign or thereafter. In view of the fresh names that now appear, it would seem that ABENEL's term of office, which may have lasted something like thirty years, came to an end.

In the 1894 Douglas Hoard there was a Hertford penny of Eadgar of the Crowned Bust type but varying from the normal in having the bust contained in the inner circle (North 751/1). The variant was noted by Grueber in the text of his report on the hoard (NC 1913, p. 9 No. 27), but was in some measure obscured by the references he cites. It was left to Prof. Michael Dolley and Dr Metcalf to bring the variety fully to notice and also to illustrate it. The mint name is clearly HIRTFOR preceded by (MO)NETA. The coin is a large fragment and the first two letters of moneta are missing, as are the last two or three letters of the moneyer's name HA ... or MA ... Grueber completes it as HANNA or MANNA, and it is likely to be something of this kind. H can be interpreted as M.

The only other specimen of this variety was thought to be in the Hunterian Museum, Glasgow, from the Coats collection; a coin found in a lot at A. H. Baldwin & Son, corresponding to the one in the Huxtable sale of 1859. Interestingly, it may, like the Douglas specimen, be attributed to Hertford. Again it is a fragment but in this case the moneyer is WULFMAER, which appears in full. Only the mint name has suffered to the extent of losing all but the final letter .. R. The coin may, however, confidently be accepted as Hertford.

The other occurrence of the moneyer WULFMAER is the reform portrait type (BMC:VI). The name occurs on a single coin of the early portrait type. This is without mint-signature but has an extra cross in the reverse field. This too may be of Hertford.

The position at this time is that Hertford had two, if not, three moneyer's operating in the same reign; ABENEL and WULFMAER, or ABENEL and HA ... or MA ..., or all three. It does not matter where one places the variant issue, Hertford was probably no longer a one moneyer mint.

We now come to Edward the Martyr (AD 975–8) for which only one type is struck, the Small Cross type (BMC:I). The diademed bust faces left, and has ANGLO after REX. The reverse has a small cross in the centre of the flan of the pattee type, the moneyer is WULFMAER – PVLFMAER MO HERT. Only this one moneyer is at work now.

During the reign of Aethelred II (978–1016) a very large output of coins came from this mint. The first coin noted is the First Hand type (BMC:iia). This coin was first seen, recorded and published by Miss van der Meer when she found it in the Berlin Cabinet. The moneyer is WULFMAER, the mint spelling is HERT. Apart from this one recording of First Hand no others have come to light, neither have the Second Hand or the Benediction Hand been recorded. An oddment that has come to light though, is a right-facing bust Crux mule. This was brought to light by B. H. I. H. Stewart in his paper 'The Early Coins of Aethelred II's Crux Issues with Right-facing Bust'. When one studies the obverse and compares it with the Benediction Hand types, it falls into place. Why? Because the moneyer is a new

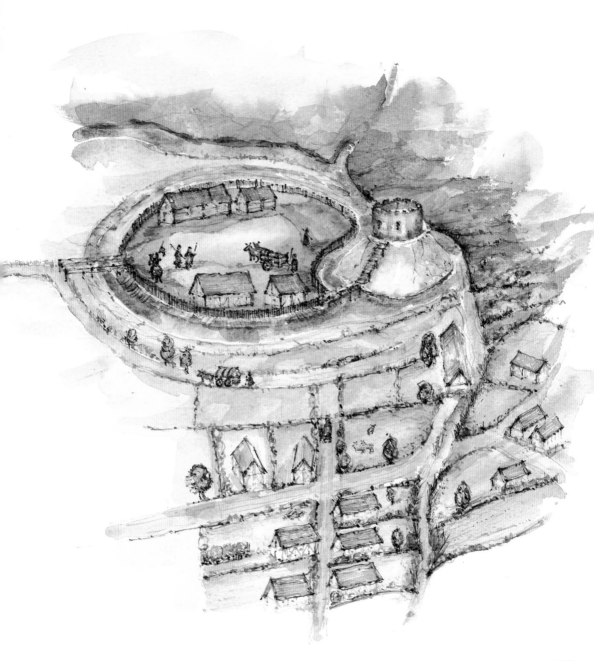

COLOUR PLATE VIII. Hertford Castle as it may have looked when first constructed in *c*.1067 – the forage parties are assembling before departing on requisition raids.

man, AETHELWERD, and the mint name is HORT.

The Crux proper (BMC:iiia) has a recording of no less than ten moneyer's to date: AELFWINE, AETHELWARD who struck both left and right-facing bust, BEORNWULF, BOIGA, LIFINC, BURINC, BYRHTLAF, EDWI, WULFNOTH, WULFRIC who struck for Edward the Martyr. Two others I have not included in the list, GODRIC and LEOFSTAN, as no full proof is at hand. A small Crux is known for Hertford. It weighs only 18 grains and is from a smaller module of dies and flans. The moneyer is BOIGA – BOGI M-O HERTF.

Of the Small Cross type (BMC:ib) two moneyers are found, WULFRIC and a new moneyer found by Miss van der Meer, MANAN M-O HVR--, and has been attributed to Hertford. This could be the same moneyer that struck the HA . . . or MA . . . coin in Eadgar's early portrait issue of Hertford!

The Long Cross issue has three moneyer's, BOIGA, GODRIC and WULFRIC. The Helmet type also has three, AELFWINE, LEOFSTAN and WULFRIC. So under Aethelred II no fewer than fourteen moneyer's were at some time employed at, or near, Hertford, in the manufacture of coin for the Great Dane Geld. The spelling of the mint name takes on quite a few forms; e.g. HIRT, HVRFT, VRF, VRTE, REFT, HEOR, HERTF and the usual HIORT. The mint signature of IORT, the H being dropped, gives rise to yet another of VRTF, all attributed to Hertford. There are comparable coins in The Fitzwilliam Collection (Sylloge 694) and from an important find of a hoard in the parish of Viby in the district of Narke in central Sweden (SHM Inv. 14935).

The Canute series I have not finished, as the entire lot for Hertford have to be re-researched; this is because of new finds and an entirely new Continental hoard.

For Harold I, two moneyer's were at work, DEORSIGE and GODMAN. They struck all the issues and many variants of the Fleur-de-Lis type (BMC:vi). Only one coin has come to light with Harthacnut's name on it. The moneyer is LEOFRED. It could possibly be a Scandinavian coin, this can only be answered if a comparable coin of this type is found elsewhere.

From Edward the Confessor (AD 1042–66) the coins can now be grouped into three-yearly intervals, from which firm dates can be fixed. There are ten types with three issues with variants. Ten moneyer's are also engaged at this mint, six on the Radiate/Small Cross type (BMC:i). Mules between the Sovereign Eagles and the Hammer Cross types (BMC:ix & xi) are more numerous to find, rather than the type proper. The moneyer's for these are SAEMAR and WILGRIP. Only GOLDWINE strikes the sole Hammer Cross.

An unusual reverse is found for Radiate/Small Cross for Hertford, although the normal is a Small Cross pattee, and quite plain. One type by SAEMAR has 'C' devices facing the ends of the centre cross. No other coin from any other mint has this device on the reverse of this type and is unique to Hertford. York is the only other mint that is different by using annulets on all the reverses of its coins.

No coins have been found for Harold II (AD 1066) relating to the Hertford Mint.

William I coins now become very scarce for this mint. The first of this reign is the Profile type (BMC:i), the moneyer is SAEMAR. The next three issues are not recorded for Hertford, the Two Stars type (BMC:v) has two moneyer's IELFRIC and THIDRIC. Only one Cross & Trefoil type (BMC: vii) is known; it is by SEMIER (SAEMAR).

If it had not been for the Beaworth Hoard (1833), where 6,439 Paxs pennies were found, Hertford would not have had a Paxs at all. Eight were found for Hertford, one by SEMIER ON HIRTF, and seven by DIEDRIC ON HRTFI (THIDRIC). This is

BMC:viii and the last for William I.

William II (Rufus) coins are also exceptionally rare. The reign starts with the Profile type (BMC:i) the moneyer is THIDRIC. Two moneyer's, IELGAR and THIDRIC, strike the next issue, Cross in Quatrefoils type (BMC:ii) of which only five are known.

Three moneyer's strike the last that we know for Hertford, the type is Cross Voided (BMC:iii): they are IELGAR, THIDRIC and SAEMAR. A very interesting mule exists between this type and what would have been the next type (BMC:v) Cross Pattee/Fleury from the obverse die only. It has been suggested that the dies were made ready but were never commissioned. This then, seems to date the closing of the mint at Hertford to about 1095 or 1096. As no other coins of any new type has yet come to light, we can safely say that the type iv was never issued. On the other hand, should anything new come to light – as at Cambridge where a coin of Henry I was found in 1978, of the type BMC:v, moneyer FRISE ON GRATA, when the mint there was thought to have finished in 1100 – it could still give hope of yet more and later coins to come from Hertford.

Of all the Anglo-Saxon and Norman coins that have been found from the mint at Hertford, a staggering 92 per cent have come from Continental hoards or collections. In some cases this can be explained. For example, the St Peter's pence to Rome, the Great Danegeld, the payment of Canute's disbanded fleet, the payment of Weregeld and so on. As to any local finds of coin from the Hertford mint, I only know of one, in a total of 64 coins. It is a Crux penny of Aethelred II. If any others have been found then they have never been recorded or declared. This is sometimes the case and is a very great pity.

Abbreviations:

BMC   *British Museum Catalogue of Coins.*
NC   *Numismatic Chronicle.*
North   North, J. J., *English Hammered Coinage.*

Reprinted with permission from *Caesaromagus*, vols. 29 & 30, 1975.

Appendix C

THE ALIEN BENEDICTINE PRIORY AT WARE
Rev. Harry P. Pollard

The following article is excerpted from *Transactions of the East Herts Archaeological Society*, vol. III part 2 (1906), by kind permission of the East Hertfordshire Archaeological Society.

Of the many historians and others who have attempted a description of the religious houses of Ware, only four, Dugdale, Tanner, Cussans and Mr. Walters, give an accurate idea of the distinction between the two establishments; Weaver, Chauncy, Parkinson, Salmon and Clutterbuck hopelessly confuse the Benedictine and Franciscan houses, and later writers have copied and added to their errors. Some have established a Franciscan house at Ware about 130 years before St. Francis lived, others have attached the Franciscan house to a Benedictine Abbey, a blunder which it is surprising that anyone with the slightest knowledge of the monks and friars could have made – no one would have more appreciated the absurdity of this unique state of affairs than the parties concerned. Parkinson, while pointing out an error of Weaver, falls into the equally glaring one of making Margaret Quincey refound a house erected some hundred years after her death, and Dugdale's ambiguous wording as to situation, together with a probable imitation of a very late Tudor window, in a malting in Baldock Street, has led to a modern building being described as the remains of a religious house which stood on a different site.

The result of these various errors has been that at the present time the prevalent idea is that Ware possessed only one Priory; as a matter of fact, however, there were two distinct establishments, the Alien Benedictine Priory being of far greater importance than the house of Friars Minor with which it is generally confused.

In the year 517 St. Evroul, Evroult or Ebrulfe, was born at Bayeux, where he lived and married; subsequently he and his wife took vows and, with three companions only, sought out a lonely spot by the River Charenton. Here St. Evroul is said to have worked miracles; his establishment escaped the Danish ravages, but in 943, under the King's orders, the ornaments and relics were taken away. The greater part of the monks followed the relics, and by the year 1043 very little appears to have remained of the house. A priest from Beauvais named Restold came, however, and dwelt at the spot, and found benefactors willing to repair the ruined church, one of whom was Geroy, a man of great valour and piety. He was succeeded by his second son, William, who gave lands and the newly restored church of St. Evroul to Bec, and became a monk at the latter house. Evroul now became a cell to Bec, inhabited by a small body of monks headed by Lanfranc, who became Archbishop of Canterbury in 1070.

The nephews of William Geroy, Hugh and Robert de Grantmesnil, wished to found a monastery near the lordship from which they took their name. Their uncle suggested, however, that they had better join with him in restoring St. Evroul; this they did. The Bec rights were exchanged and the new St. Evroul arose with the full license of Duke William, of Archbishop Malger, and of the other Norman prelates. Theodoric, the first abbot of the new foundation, was succeeded by Robert de Grantmesnil, who had become a monk of this house. A few years after Robert was deposed or driven to resign by Duke William.

One of those who accompanied Duke William to England in 1066 was Hugh de Grantmesnil, who became possessed of lands in Ware and many other places. Some of this property he gave to the Abbey he had helped to restore. A copy of the Charter of William the Conqueror confirming these gifts is given by Dugdale, part of which reads as follows: 'He gave ... three villeins of Ware ... He gave also the church of Ware and all tenths which belonged to it and two carucates of land ...' The priory founded by Hugh de Grantmesnil probably consisted of a cloister and a few buildings near it, of simple construction, having some thirty inhabitants.

By the establishment of these Alien Priories much English money was sent abroad without any return being made, for the foreign abbeys made no provision for the district which benefited them, save placing a few dependent monks on the property to look after the estates and remit the profits. Little is known with regard to the inmates of these houses; it is uncertain whether they were all Frenchmen, and perhaps in some cases consisted of a French prior with a few English monks. The Priory of Ware was one of the more important alien houses, as its Prior was Proctor of the English possessions of St. Evroul, which included, in addition to the Ware property, lands at Hailes and other property in Gloucestershire; in Northamptonshire the manor and church of Byfield, a pension from Eydon Rectory, the manor, impropriate rectory and advowson of Marston St. Laurence, the manor and advowson of Middleton Chenduit, the impropriate rectory of Radstone; in Leicestershire, lands at Belgrave, Shevesby and East Shilton; in Warwickshire, lands at Over Pillarton; also property in the following places: Meldreth, Wilcote, Hemingby, London, Charlton, Peatling and Stainton by Langworth and the benefices of Carleton Curly, Rock, Burton Novery, Midelynton, Dersford, North Middleton, Thurcaston and Glenfield. Unfortunately this list is not complete.

Under King John all the alien priories to the number of eighty-one were sequestrated and their revenues taken for the King's necessities. Soon after the death of John probably the great hall, chapel and other rooms of the Priory were erected by Margaret de Quincey.

In 1228 the parishioners of Ware complained to Gregory IX stating that the Prior had refused to let the cure of their Parish Church be served by a sufficient vicar, to the grievance and prejudice of the said church and parishioners. He received from the Vicar an annual pension of ten marks, and reserved to himself the tithes of the mills of the whole parish of Ware and Thundridge, also the tithes of the park and woods of Robert, Earl of Leicester, and the tithes also of corn and hay of the said parish to the prejudice and more destruction of the said vicarage. The Pope issued a mandatory letter to the Bishop and Dean of London to hear and determine the matter and the Prior and men of Ware having first sworn that they would stand by the award without appeal, the dispute was settled in the following manner. The Prior, William, having shown his letters of authority to the satisfaction of the Bishop and Dean, declared, for himself and for his successors, that the then Vicar, Nicholas Speleman, and his successors, would be released from payment of the pension, and it was ordained that, if the Prior or his successors should attempt to claim the pension, the tithes should, from that time, remain to the said Vicar and his successors for ever. The vicarage was endowed as follows. The Vicar and others appointed Vicars in the same Church, shall take possession of all the small tenths and oblations whatsoever with all things belonging to the said Church of Ware and Chapel of Thundridge (except tenths of sheaves of corn and of hay, exclusive of the tenths of hay due to the Vicar and his successors from the farm of Robert of the Park, Sylvester of the Water, and Walter Clerk). The Vicar was also to have tenths of wood of trees, of underwood, wild trees, groves and dells, and all hedges of the parish town of Ware and Thundridge, tenths of timber and bark, growing crops, fruit, wool, lambs, pigs, geese, swans, calves, cheese, butter, milk, agistment, animals, stags, rabbits, fish and of all fowl, mills, business, profit and principal inns, and all other things belonging to the altars of the Church of Ware and Chapel of Thundridge. The Vicar is also to have 'a messuage, that is called the Priest's Messuage, together with the increase therefrom arising which was the Priory's, and he shall sustain the ordinary burdens of the aforesaid Church . . .'

This endowment, with the consent of all parties, was confirmed by Roger Niger in 1231 with the clause 'and in like manner of the tenths of sheaves, growing crops and hay of the farm of Richard de Ware Senior shall remain to the aforesaid Vicar in perpetuity'.

The Vicar of Ware appears to have become a person of importance, for in a very much mutilated deed of the year 1240 in the British Museum, something, possibly a sum of £500, was in the hand of Sir Anketil, Vicar of Ware.

At an Assize held at Hertford before John de Reygate and others in 1278, the Prior of Ware for one carucate of land in the same town was ordered to make two bridges, one in Lumpwellesmade, ten feet long and six feet wide; the other in ffoueracremade, ten feet long and six feet wide.

In the year 1283 Hawise Wake applied to the King for the recovery of property which her ancestors had given to the Priory. As Hawise was a most important person it is necessary to trace her descent from the founder of the priory clearly. Petronilla (great-granddaughter of Hugh de Grantmesnil) married Robert, Earl of Leicester, who confirmed to St. Evroul the donation of Hugh de Grantmesnil; Margaret, the younger daughter of this Robert, married Saier de Quincey, Earl of Winchester; Saier had four children, Roger, William, Robert and Hawise; Robert had the manor of Ware by gift, which ultimately came to this third daughter, Hawise, who married Baldwin de Wake.

From an Assize roll of the year 1283 it appears that Hawise Wake states that her ancestors have given and granted lands and tenements to the Priory of Ware, which is of the foundation of her said ancestors, that there was a residence and storehouse within the enclosure of the Priory, which the said ancestors had access to whenever they required, that lately the lands and tenements of the deceased Johanna de Bohun (sister of Hawise) have been taken into the King's hands, and Hawise wishes them to be restored to her. Also that Margaret, sometime Countess of Winchester, whenever she pleased, stayed in the aforesaid Priory of Ware, and in the same Priory constructed a great hall, and a great chamber, and a chapel, and that the aforesaid Countess held her tenant's courts in the aforesaid hall at such times as were pleasing to her without any impediment whatever; that after her death her son William held his courts of the Manor of Ware at his will in the aforesaid hall, and subsequently gave the Manor of Ware to Robert de Quincey his brother, who did the same as the aforesaid Count and Margaret at his pleasure.

In the year 1290 there appears to have been a dispute concerning common of pasture between the free tenants of Charwelton and those of Byfield. The cause of the Charwelton inhabitants was championed by the Abbot of Biddlesdon, that of the Byfield inhabitants by the Lord of the Manor, Brother John, Prior of Ware; the covenant in settlement is in the British Museum.

In the general ecclesiastical taxation of the clergy within the Diocese of London made about 1291, the entries relating to the Prior of Ware are as follows:

In Parish of Saint Dionis (Back Church) 20s., thence tenths 2s.
Church of Ware, 60 marks.
Tenths, £4.
Medr (1/20), 40s.

In 1293 a war began between England and France lasting some five years and the second seizure took place of the alien priories, which at this time numbered nearly one hundred; the King, Edward I, lest the alien monks should be of any assistance to his enemies, moved them twenty miles from the seaboard. Ware, being some thirty-five miles, was naturally unaffected by this removal.

On the pretext of every new French war the same process of sequestration was repeated by the following sovreigns, and the revenues of the sequestrated houses went to pay the army and for other purposes.

The history of the alien priory of Ware, as a religious house, ends in 1414, in which year all the alien priories in England were suppressed by an Act of Parliament held at Leicester. Thus, after a troubled existence of some 330 years, came to an end one of those establishments which were centres of true education, hospitality and almsgiving. It is worth notice that no charges were made against the monks; but that the reason for the suppression was that the revenues of these houses were enriching France, with whom England was constantly at war.

It would be of great interest to learn what became of the Ware brethren, whether they returned to France or not; unfortunately very little is known respecting the dissolution of the alien priories in general and with regard to Ware there appears to be no information at all.

The King in 1416 gave the alien proctorial house or Priory of Ware to the Carthusian Priory of Sheene. At an Inquisition taken at Ware, January 3rd, 1425, however, it is stated that Thomas, Earl of Salisbury, held the advowson of the Priory Church of Ware; if the King did take the Priory away from Sheene it was probably only for a very short period, as the latter house continued to present to the living until the time of Henry VIII; this King, after the dissolution of Sheene in 1540, presented the Ware property to Trinity College, Cambridge, in 1546. The reference to Ware in the Charter of Endowment dated December 24th 1546, is as follows: To hold all that our Rectory and Church of Ware in our County of Hertford, with its jurisdiction of all parts and belongings lately pertaining and belonging to the Monastery of Sheene, in our County of Surrey, now not long since dissolved.

In the British Museum is the seal of Prior John, A.D. 1260; it is of dark-green wax, the edge injured, originally fine; $1\frac{3}{4}$" x 1"; the shape is a pointed oval. The Prior is shown with embroidered vestments, standing on a corbel, holding a book. Inscription: + S JOHANNIS: PRIORIS DE WARE.

Clutterbuck has an illustration of two others: (1) a seal of Prior Ralph (fourteenth century), about $1\frac{3}{4}$" x 1" when perfect, pointed oval, in a double niche, with canopy broken away; two saints, with hands broken off, standing, one on the left with key, the other on the right with pastoral staff. In the field on each side three roses. In base, under a pointed arch, the Prior kneeling in prayer to the right. Inscription, M RADULPH . . . ORIS DE . . . A sulphur cast of this is in the British Museum. (2) A seal of Prior John (fourteenth century?), pointed oval, in double niche with elaborate canopy; two saints standing, one on the left with key in left hand, book in right, the other on right with pastoral staff in right hand, book in left; in base, under a round-headed arch, the Priory kneeling in prayer to the left.

The Priory buildings would consist of a cloister with dormitory on the east, and guest-house, frater chapel, great hall, Prior's lodging, infirmary and other buildings near the other sides; without excavation the sites cannot be fixed with certainty, neither is it known where the monks' cemetery was; but there is a Dead Lane running from the north-east corner of the churchyard south-east to High Street, as there is also a Dead Lane close to the Priory at Hitchin and another close to Royston Priory; this may afford some clue to the cemetery site. At the present time an iron tablet at each end of Dead Lane untruthfully informs the visitor that the lane is 'Church Street'.

Until the end of May, 1906, there was no certainty as to the site, although as before mentioned there were several random guesses. There appears to be nothing at the British Museum or Record Office to indicate the site of the Priory, and the Vice-Master of Trinity, Dr. W. Aldis Wright, to whom I am much indebted for the search he has made, has been unable to discover anything to throw light on the site of the Priory in the records at the College, and suggested local enquiry. After having seen maps showing the position of the College property, and having been told that there was an idea that the old Rectory, now known as the Manor House, was a priory (this suggestion however, appears to be of very modern origin, as in the College records this house is always called the Rectory), I inspected the house, by kind permission of Dr. Boyd, and am of opinion that it was probably a building standing at the south-east angle of the cloisters, and that the upper floor, which contains some very early woodwork, was the dormitory of the alien priory. The house is nearly entirely constructed of oak, and roughly in the shape of a letter L reversed, the long portion running north and south.

The area of the land on the north side of the churchyard on which the Schools and Rectory stand is a sufficient indication that this is the site of the Benedictine Priory, as the other portions of the College property are too unsuitable both as regards situation and size.

LIST OF PRIORS

The list is unfortunately very defective, the name of the earliest prior at present known being some 150 years after the foundation of the house.

William	here in	1228
John	" "	1260
Ralph	" "	14th century
John Gerand	" "	1371
William Herbert	" "	1377 & 1381
Nicholas Champeney, last prior	" "	1409
Dissolution	" "	1414

Reprinted with permission from *Transactions of the East Herts. Archaeol. Soc.*, vol. III, pt I, 1906.

Appendix D

'HOW DOES THE PORTRAYAL OF THE VIKINGS COMPARE WITH THE REALITY IN HERTFORDSHIRE?'
Richard Wilson

THE EVENTS OF AD 895

The Anglo-Saxon Chronicle entries are really the only source of material for this incident. Later writers such as Henry of Huntingdon, Chauncy, Salmon, Scott of Amwell (poet), and in particular Turnor in his *History of Hertford* published in 1830, have created a myth for either religious i.e. anti-Danish reasons, or to produce a good story. Turnor's account is the culmination of this process.

His story has the Danes of Ware laying waste the countryside and burning down Hertford. They built a fort and weir (thus Ware) and penetrated as far as Port Hill, Hertford where there was a natural harbour. Alfred, to defeat the Danes, carried out major engineering works on the Lea diverting the river into three channels at Waltham, after which he shut out the tides at Blackwall by means of sluice gates, thus stranding the Danish Fleet all along the river's course!

There is simply no evidence to support Turnor's story.

The archaeological record can be summarized as follows:

1. A Viking sword found at Hertford but attributed to a later period.
2. A bodkin talisman, made from antler, found at Ware Lock. Probably Viking.
3. A reputed Viking ship found at Hertford Sele Mill, but it could be any age.

4.   Reputed ship's timbers found at Stanstead Abbots. Again could be any age.
5.   Some fortifications on Widbury Hill. Age unknown.

We are left therefore with the Anglo-Saxon Chronicle to answer two questions. What were the Danes up to and what was the significance of the events of AD 895? Where exactly was the Danish camp on the Lea?

WHAT WERE THE DANES UP TO?

According to the Chronicle, a Danish force of eighty ships headed by a Chieftain called Hastein, Hastings or Hasten, landed in Kent in AD 892 overrunning a half-built Saxon fort and building one at Milton. Hastein's party was the second wave of a larger force of 250 ships. This 'great army' had come across the channel from Boulogne after suffering stiff resistance on the Continent, maybe Alfred's England was half-defended; easy pickings? H. R. Loyn: *Anglo-Saxon England and the Normans* (1962)) believes that this invasion, aided and abetted by the Danes in East Anglia and Northumbria, was part of a concerted attempt to overthrow Alfred's kingdom. They failed; organization and systematic defence defeated them.

893: The Danes leave their forts in Kent to head across the Thames and into Essex with their booty. Alfred intercepts them at Farnham and recovers the booty, following the Danes to besiege them on an islet (Thorney?) in the River Colne. Native Danes from Northumbria and East Anglia distract Alfred by besieging Exeter and 'a fortification on the north-east of Devon'. The Chronicle is confusing here because from Thorney Island on the Colne, the Danes are suddenly transported to Benfleet in Essex without explanation. The Chronicle explicitly states that the Danes stayed on Thorney when the English went off to defend Exeter, because their king had been wounded. One can only assume that he got better, and decided to go to Benfleet. A detachment of Alfred's army and a contingent of Londoners rout the Danes at Benfleet, capturing Hastein's family, returning them only when Hastein promises not to attack them any more. This promise is broken immediately. Hastein carried on pillaging, regrouping at Shoebury in Essex with reinforcements from the native Danes. The force heads west and builds a fort at Buttington, on the Severn. Here they are besieged by the Saxons and routed again. The survivors regroup again within Essex with native reinforcements. They then returned west-wards and built a fort at Chester, where they are again besieged.

894: The Danes leave Chester to plunder in Wales, returning to Essex through Danish territory and resting in Mersea before finally sailing along the Thames and up the Lea.

895: The 'Ware episode'. Danes then head for Bridgnorth on Severn, still well within the borders of Alfred's part of England, where they build another fort. The Danes are pursued by the English.

896: Danish army disperses. 'The Viking army had not by God's grace afflicted the English people to a very great extent . . .'

Whether or not the Danes were successful depends on what their aims were. If, as Loyn believes, they intended to overthrow Alfred, then they were of course unsuccessful. Yet this thesis is not entirely convincing. If the force that landed in Kent was a conquering army, they do not seem to have behaved like one. From the outset they fought a guerrilla campaign, for the most part assiduously avoiding Alfred's standing army. They fought Alfred only when they had to: when they were intercepted at Farnham, when they were attacked at Benfleet and Buttington. Each time they were defeated. They made no attempt to capture strategic positions, like the City of London. They behaved, in short, like opportunistic pirates. While in Kent, they travelled in small plundering bands, until the Saxons caught up with them. They moved haphazardly, back and forth all over the country in the space of a few months, grabbing all the loot they could get. If conquest was their intention, they had a very strange way of going about it. Thus they dispersed in 896 because they had got what they wanted. Alfred, too, was tightening up his defences against their activities. Perhaps ultimately the Danes were perversely responsible for the strengthening and reorganization of local government in England: their very presence was an incentive for the kingdom to be well managed and efficiently run.

WHERE WAS THE DANISH CAMP ON THE LEA?

The most popular candidate for the Danish camp is Widbury Hill, which overlooks the Lea between Ware and Stanstead Abbots. Here it is easy to slip into romanticism; it looks and feels like the right sort of place for a Viking fort even today. The most articulate argument in favour of this site came from Mr Eliot Howard, quoted in the *Hertfordshire Mercury* in 1911. Together with the Buxtons (prominent local landowners), he surveyed the site and claimed to have found 'the remains of a deep ditch along the crown of the hill extending about 120 yards along the side of the field and then apparently turning inwards'. When I took a look for myself, I could find nothing that matched this description. The aerial photographs were similarly disappointing. This could of course be because the area has been well ploughed since 1911. Nowadays Ordnance Survey maps record a 'fort' there, but that in itself does not really prove anything. No archaeological relics have been found there. A more compelling argument is that of place-name evidence.

It is known that the name occurs as *Witteberwe* in 1308 and also that the 'bury' comes either from '*beorg*' (barrow/hill) or '*burgh*' (fort). The '*Wid*' element refers to the white chalk rockface on the hill. The English Place-name Society believe that the 'bury' element means 'hill' rather than fort; it is not clear whether or not they were aware of the historical debate, but it seems impossible to be certain one way or the other. Perhaps the most convincing argument is Howard's observation of the position of the hill: 'It commands extensive views of the upper Lea valley and all the neighbourhood round. It is opposite the 20th. and 21st. milestone on the Ermyn Street road from London. It would command the road and the ford at Ware . . . It lies just inside the Danelaw . . .'

To this one would add that it seems to be the highest hill above the Lea for several miles around; strategically ideal for a fort, well placed to withstand the initial Saxon onslaught. Widbury hill might seem to fit closest the description 'twenty miles above the City of London'. I toyed with the idea that 'Stanstead' (which lies exactly 20 miles north of London) may have originally been 'Hastaen's Stead', but the English Place-name Society tell me that the name was originally 'Stane Stead', meaning 'Stone' stead. Perhaps here is where the Viking 'bodkin' from Ware comes in. It was found, after all, next to the point at which Ermine Street crosses the Lea. Perhaps that was where the fort was. Although measurement cannot have been exact, it seems fair to assume that the 'twenty miles' did probably relate to Ermine Street. On the other hand, when one looks at the Anglo-Saxon Chronicle, the fort on the Lea is unique because it is described by its distance from London rather than the place it is built on. This implies that the fort was built outside an inhabited place. If one wants to assume that the fort was built on a hill, then Widbury is as good as any, but Port Hill in Hertford, another contender, is similarly well placed. Port Hill has the apparent added weight of having Danesbury Cricket Ground on its crown, although that naming could simply stem from popular mythology. The fact is that there is so little evidence that the whole debate is just speculation. It is really a question of whatever you want to believe. The outstanding ambiguities are as follows:

1. The problem of 'twenty miles north of London' – how accurately were they measuring this distance? Why did they not mention Ware or Hertford if they were in existence at this time? The river Lea bends westwards at just over twenty miles north of London. Virtually any point from Stanstead Abbots to Hertford could roughly fit the description.
2. Whereabouts would the Danes want to build a fort? In a settlement or out in the middle of nowhere – on a hill or in a wood?
3. What was the state of Ware in 895? A Saxon settlement (being on the north-eastern side of the Lea) would have fallen inside the Danelaw after 886, the date of the Treaty of Wedmore which set out the Saxon–Danish boundary. Does this mean that Ware was at the Danes' disposal; or a likely site for a base?

In the absence of firm evidence, it seems safest simply to say that the site probably lies somewhere beside the Lea, between Stanstead Abbots and Hertford.

List of Significant Excavations 1952-1993

In addition to those plotted and numbered on the aerial photographs (see Front and Back endpapers), many other smaller excavations, rescue and recording operations and watching briefs were undertaken. These are too numerous to list individually but most produced some evidence. Where possible the excavations are listed in chronological sequence and the synopsis is arranged in the following order: Number on photographic plot; Excavating body; Director; Finds; Publications; Present location of finds (this, unless otherwise stated, is also where the excavation records are lodged). The following abbreviations are used: HAU Hart Archaeological Unit; HAT Hertfordshire Archaeological Trust; HM Hertford Museum; WM Ware Museum.

WARE

1. **1952.** John Holmes *et al.* Section excavated across the Roman Ermine Street on the south side of the Meads. *Finds:* The Ermine Street, side ditches, various types of Roman pottery and artefacts. *Publication: Trans. East Herts. Archaeol. Soc.* 13 pt 2. 1954. *Finds location:* HM.

2. **1954.** Mr Eddie Barkes. Observed and recorded structural remains during sewer pipe work in the Priory grounds. *Finds:* Structural elements of the Franciscan Friary. *Publication:* see entry No. 6.

3. **1974.** HAU/HM. Martin Petchey. Section across Roman Ermine Street on south side of river Lea. *Finds:* The Ermine Street, side ditches and remains of a chalk-floored building. Many Roman coins, pottery and other artefacts. A cremation burial containing Romano-Saxon pottery. An antler bodkin, or talisman, of Saxo-Viking date. *Publication:* Unpublished. *Finds location:* HM/WM.

4. **1976.** HAU. Clive Partridge. Emergency rescue excavations during construction of Flood Relief Scheme on the south side of Ware Lock. *Finds:* Roman pottery, coins and other artefacts including an iron slave shackle. Structural elements including chalk platforms for buildings. *Publication: Herts. Archaeology* 7, 1979. *Finds location:* HM/WM.

5. **1976-80.** HAU. Clive Partridge. Detailed examination of the remains of a small Roman town, at Allen & Hanbury's (Glaxo UK). *Finds:* Many hundreds of coins, artefacts and pottery types. A Roman pottery kiln, inhumation and cremation burials and the Roman Ermine Street and Military Way. Prehistoric remains of Mesolithic, Neolithic and Bronze Age date. Late Iron Age occupation, ditches, pits, pottery and coins. *Publication:* Awaiting publication. *Finds location:* HAT/WM/Glaxo UK.

6. **1977.** HAU. Clive Partridge. Observation and rescue recording during the laying of replacement sewer pipes in the Priory grounds. *Finds:* Various structural elements believed to be the remains of the Franciscan Friary Church (see also entry No. 2). Several contemporary inhumation burials also recorded. *Publication: Herts. Archaeology* 7, 1979. *Finds location:* None recovered.

7. **1977.** HAU. Ivan Day. Emergency rescue excavations during sewer replacement in Buryfield. *Finds:* Late Iron Age ditches and pottery. Roman burials with associated pottery. *Publication: Herts. Archaeology* 7, 1979. *Finds location:* HM.

8. **1977.** HAU. Ivan Day. Emergency excavations on the site of new extension to Ware Library. *Finds:* Roman features with pottery and coins. Structural evidence and pottery of fifth–seventh-century date. Medieval and post-Medieval structures and pottery. *Publication: Herts. Archaeology 7, 1979. Finds location:* HM.

9. **1979.** HAU. Ivan Day. Excavations in advance of development at White Swan Yard. *Finds:* A Late Iron Age ditch with contemporary pottery. Medieval and post-Medieval structures. *Publication: Herts. Archaeology 7, 1979. Finds location:* HM.

10. **1979.** HAU. Fred Crosby. Small investigation after demolition of Medieval building on the north-west side of Church Street. *Finds:* Mainly debris of Medieval and post-Medieval date. Remains of a small fourteenth-century cellar where the wall facing was composed of tightly packed cattle bones. *Publication:* Unpublished. *Finds location:* HAT.

11. **1980.** HAU. Hugh Borrill. Excavations in St Marys Churchyard. *Finds:* To the north of the church many burials dating from the seventeenth-century. Just to the north of the present bell tower a large bell pit of twelfth–thirteenth-century date. Some thirteenth-century pottery, and several Nuremberg jettons of sixteenth-century date. *Publication: Herts. Archaeology 8, 1980–82. Finds location:* HAT.

12. **1981.** HAU. Ivan Day & Clive Partridge. Excavation during partial demolition and restoration work on thirteenth-century building at 3 West Street. *Finds:* Much information about the structural history of the building. A series of hearths, ranging from a thirteenth-century open central hearth to an elaborate late Tudor fireplace. In the yard to the rear of the building an Iron Age ditch with contemporary pottery and artefacts. A Saxon *sceatta* (small silver penny) of sixth-century date. *Publication: Herts. Archaeology 8, 1980–82. Finds location:* Returned to owners (except the Saxon *sceatta* which is in Ware Museum).

13. **1982.** HAU. Clive Partridge. Major rescue excavation behind 13–23 Baldock Street (west side). *Finds:* Late Iron Age features and pottery. Several Roman pits and ditches with contemporary pottery and artefacts. Traces of late Saxon timber buildings with some contemporary pottery. *Publication:* Unpublished. *Finds location:* HAT.

14. **1983.** HAU. Hugh Borrill & Peter Cottis. Excavations in advance of redevelopment at Waggoners Yard on the east side of Baldock Street. *Finds:* A few shallow early prehistoric features with associated flintwork. Much of the area had been disturbed by a large Second World War air raid shelter. Some small pits containing grass-tempered and plain sandy-ware of late Saxon date. Several large pits containing thirteenth-century pottery and post-hole evidence of buildings. The ancient watercourse of the Upper Bourne was found to be enclosed in a Victorian brick culvert. *Publication:* Unpublished. *Finds location:* HAT.

15. **1984–5.** HAU. Clive Partridge. Emergency excavation on the site of the old Pastille Building during construction of a new store building (N12 on Glaxo site plan). *Finds:* Good section of Roman Ermine Street and underlying Military Way. Many truncated remains of Iron Age ditches, Roman ditches, pits and several wells. Iron Age and Roman pottery, Roman coins and artefacts. *Publication:* Awaiting publication. *Finds location:* HAT.

16. **1985.** HAU. Peter Cottis & Donald Stewart. Exploratory excavation in the northern part of the 'Old Manor house' gardens, on the probable site of the Alien Benedictine Priory. *Finds:* Some indeterminate sub-surface features, cobbled surfaces and fragments of structural evidence for possible walkways or cloister structures. The area had been much disturbed by gardening activities. *Publication:* Unpublished. *Finds location:* HAT.

17. **1985.** HAU. Donald Stewart. Investigation and recording of waterside structures and sunken vessels in the 'Old Barge Cut', adjacent to Glaxo's Sports and Social Club. *Finds:* Many partly waterlogged and silted-up remains of landing stages and barges. *Publication:* Unpublished. *Finds location:* HAT.

18. **1987.** HAT. Simon McCudden. Excavations in the south-west sector of Glaxo's, between Priory Street and Harris's Lane. *Finds:* Mainly Roman pits, ditches and gullies of 'back-garden type' occupation. One or two scrappy inhumations. Little structural evidence. *Publication:* Preliminary report for Developers. *Finds location:* HAT.

19. **1987.** HAT. Nicola Goodwin & Adrian Havercroft. Exploratory excavations in an area behind 65–83 High Street including the 'Secret Garden' site. *Finds:* Mainly finds of twelfth–fourteenth-century date. A deposit of fifteenth-century leatherwork was found in one area. Some Roman pottery and artefacts. Remains of riverside structures of possible Saxon date and a bronze strap end with silver inlay of sixth–eighth-century date. *Publication:* Preliminary report for Developer. *Finds location:* HAT.

20. **1988.** HAT. Simon McCuddon. Evaluation excavation on the site of the old Chaseside Works. *Finds:* Evidence for occupation of twelfth–fourteenth-centuries. *Publication:* Unpublished. *Finds location:* HAT.

21. **1989.** HAT. Nicola Godwin. Preliminary excavations behind 49 Baldock Street. *Finds:* The area had been badly disturbed previously. Some Medieval greyware pottery. *Publication:* Unpublished. *Finds location:* HAT.

22. **1989.** HAT. Nicola Godwin. Excavations in advance of extension to building P11 (see Glaxo site plan) at Glaxo's. *Finds:* Roman Ermine Street and extensive structural remains to the east and west of the street. Roman pottery, coins and artefacts. *Publication:* Preliminary report for Developers. *Finds location:* HAT.

23. **1990–92.** HAT. Hester Cooper-Reade. Excavation on south side of Priory Street at Millside, Glaxo's, in advance of car park construction. *Finds:* Some evidence for Roman occupation, including chalk raft foundations (similar to those found on the south side of the Lea and at Ware Lock). *Publication:* Preliminary report for Developers. *Finds location:* HAT.

24. **1993.** HAT. C. Walker. Exploratory excavations on part of the Buryfield at Ware Football Club. *Finds:* Late Roman levels with scatter of Roman pottery and artefacts. *Publication:* Preliminary report for Developer. *Finds location:* HAT.

HERTFORD

1. **1973.** HM. Martin Petchey. Exploratory excavations on part of the Railway Street old car park site. *Finds:* Large ditch running north–south across Bircherley Green believed to be the tenth-century *burghal* ditch. Saxo-Norman and

twelfth-century pottery from ditch fill. *Publication: Herts. Archaeology* 5, 1977. *Finds location:* HM.

2. **1973.** HM. Martin Petchey. Excavation on the line of Castle walls and ditches, behind 12–14 Parliament Square. *Finds:* Medieval Castle defences. A scatter of Medieval and post-Medieval pottery and some Saxo-Norman sherds. *Publication: Herts. Archaeology* 5, 1977. *Finds location:* HM.

3. **1974.** HM/HAU. Martin Petchey. Excavations before redevelopment of Castle Hall site. *Finds:* Castle moat profiles. Remains of flax retting features. Sole and leather fragments from Medieval shoes. Medieval and post-Medieval pottery. *Publication: Herts. Archaeology* 5, 1977. *Finds location:* HM.

4. **1977–78.** HAU. Charles Hill. Excavation before redevelopment on west side of Honey Lane. *Finds:* Many structural remains of early–late Medieval buildings. Wells, pits and cobbled surfaces. Quantities of Saxo-Norman, Medieval and post-Medieval pottery. Several inhumation burials belonging to cemetery discovered in adjacent Market Square. *Publication:* Unpublished. *Finds location:* HAT.

5. **1979–80.** HAU. Clive Partridge, Ivan Day, Hugh Borrill. Extensive excavations on the site of town centre redevelopment at Bircherley Green. *Finds:* Further section of the tenth-century *burghal* ditch. Structural remains, on the Railway Street frontages, of late Saxon date with associated pottery and artefacts. Remains of Medieval structures and much Medieval and post-Medieval pottery. *Publication:* Unpublished. *Finds location:* HAT.

6. **1980.** HAU. Hugh Borrill. Excavations on the site of the old Covered Market. *Finds:* Some remains of earlier buildings. A late Medieval lime kiln. A scatter of Saxo-Norman, Medieval and post-Medieval pottery. *Publication:* Unpublished. *Finds location:* HAT.

7. **1980.** HAU. Ivan Day. Exploratory excavation before redevelopment on the Museum car park site. *Finds:* A scatter of mainly Medieval and post-Medieval material. Little structural evidence. *Publication:* Unpublished. *Finds location:* HAT.

8. **1980.** HAU. Ivan Day. Rescue work on the site of an extension at the back of Canvas Holidays, in Bull Plain. *Finds:* Several small pits and shallow linear features. Sherds of Saxo-Norman and early Medieval pottery. *Publication:* Unpublished. *Finds location:* HAT.

9. **1980.** HAU. Ivan Day & Hugh Borrill. Excavations and watching brief during redevelopment of the old Botsfords builder's yard on the east and north-east side of Bircherley Green. *Finds:* Several large, disturbed groups of Medieval and post-Medieval pits containing associated pottery. Remains of Medieval houses. *Publication:* Unpublished. *Finds location:* HAT.

10. **1988.** HAT. Simon McCudden & Hester Cooper-Reade. Excavations in advance of redevelopment on the old Express Dairy site. *Finds:* Sections of the Castle double moat. Occupation on the outer bailey side. Saxo-Norman and Medieval pottery. Masonry structure between the moats. *Publication:* Unpublished. *Finds location:* HAT.

11. **1988–90.** HAT. Ian Stewart & Hester Cooper-Reade. Excavations in advance of redevelopment at Millbridge/Old Cross. *Finds:* Late Iron Age/Roman features. Cremation burial *c.* AD 40–50; Roman samian pottery. Remains of wooden structure or bridge. Some Saxo-Norman and Medieval pottery. Remains of Medieval and post-Medieval buildings. *Publication:* Preliminary report for Developer. *Finds location:* HAT.

12. **1990.** HAT. C. Walker. Exploratory excavation behind 4–6 St Andrew Street. *Finds:* Many pits with pottery of twelfth–fourteenth-century date. *Publication:* Preliminary report for Developer. *Finds location:* HAT.

13. **1990.** HAT. Hester Cooper-Reade. Exploratory excavations to the rear of 54 St Andrew Street. *Finds:* Some occupation layers and pits with evidence for Late Iron Age and Roman occupation. Some Late Iron Age 'grog' tempered pottery and Roman sherds. *Publication:* Preliminary report for Developer. *Finds location:* HAT.

14. **1990.** HAT. Hester Cooper-Reade & Charles Walker. Excavation in advance of redevelopment in the old Jewsons Yard. *Finds:* Remains of the parish church of St John, with associated cemeteries. A bell casting pit. Possible fragments of the monastic structure of St Mary's Priory. Medieval and post-Medieval pottery. *Publication: Herts. Past* 29, 1990. *Finds location:* HAT.

OTHER SITES

The locations of other important sites, mentioned in the text but outside the area of the town plots, are shown on Fig. 4, with the exception of Skeleton Green, Puckeridge, which lies some seven miles north-east of Ware.

A. **1968.** East Herts. Excavation Group. Robert Kiln. Rescue excavations at Moles Farm. *Finds:* Late Bronze Age/Early Iron Age pottery, ditches and pits. Many butchered animal bones and pot boilers. *Publication: Herts. Archaeology* 2, 1970. *Finds location:* HM.

B. **1972.** East Herts. Excavation Group. Robert Kiln. Rescue excavations at Rush Green. *Finds:* Section of Roman Ermine Street. A few sherds of Prehistoric and Roman pottery. *Publication: Herts. Archaeology* 5, 1977. *Finds location:* Not retained.

C. **1976–84.** HAU. Clive Partridge. Extensive excavations in advance of gravel extraction at Foxholes Farm. *Finds:* Important remains of Neolithic, Bronze Age, Iron Age, Roman and Saxon occupation. *Publication:* Clive Partridge: *Foxholes Farm – A Multi-Period Gravel Site*, Monograph No.1. Hertfordshire Archaeological Trust, 1989. *Finds location:* HAT.

D. **1969–72** (not shown on Fig. 4). East Herts. Excavation Group. Clive Partridge. Major rescue excavations in advance of roadworks at Skeleton Green, Puckeridge. *Finds:* Extensive Late Iron Age settlement and Roman town. Many hundreds of Late Iron Age and Roman artefacts. Important structural remains including Late Iron Age buildings, pits and wells, Roman roads, buildings and ditches. *Publication:* Clive Partridge: *Skeleton Green – A Late Iron Age and Romano-British Site*, Britannia Monograph No. 2, Society for the Promotion of Roman Studies, 1981. *Finds Location:* British Museum and HAT.

Book List and Local Organizations

The publications listed below are mainly of local interest. They will be found in the Local History section at your nearest library, or can be obtained from your local bookshop. This is only a selection of the more popular or widely available literature. For the more serious student of local history, Hertford Museum and the Local Studies Section of the County Record Office (at County Hall Hertford) are mines of fascinating information.

The History of Ware, Edith Hunt (Stephen Austin & Sons, revised edition 1986)
The History of Hertford, Dr Frances Page (reprinted 1993 by Hertford Town Council, The Castle, Hertford).
The Book of Ware, Cyril Heath (Barracuda Books, 1977)
The Book of Hertford, Cyril Heath (Barracuda Books, 1977)
Yesterday's Town – Hertford, Cyril Heath (Barracuda Books, 1981)
Ware's Past in Pictures, Maurice Edwards and David Perman
(The Rockingham Press, 1991)
History in the Streets of Ware, Thera Alcock (Ware Museum Publications, 1988)
Hertford's Past in Pictures, Len Green (The Rockingham Press, 1993)

The following local organizations welcome new members and have their own publications.

East Herts. Archaeological Society (*Hertfordshire Archaeology*). Sec: Molly Redman, 1 Marsh Lane, Stanstead Abbots, SG12 8HH.
Hertfordshire Association for Local History (*Hertfordshire's Past*). Sec: Daphne Wright, Hawthornes, The Causeway, Therfield, SG8 9PP.
Hertford & Ware Local History Society (newsletters and occasional publications). Sec: Alan Greening, 3 Watermill Lane, Bengeo, SG14 3LB.
Hertford Civic Society (newsletters and occasional publications). Sec: Andrew Sangster, 25 West Street, Hertford, SG13 8EX.
The Ware Society (newsletters and occasional publications). Sec: Ralph Rudd, 13 Peter Wood Hill, Ware, SG12 9NR.
Ware Museum Trust (newsletters and publications). Sec: David Perman, 11 Musley Lane, Ware, SG12 7EN.